KANT
TODAY

KANT TODAY

TODAY

A SURVEY

ERICH PRZYWARA

TRANSLATED BY DAVID AUGUSTINE
INTRODUCTION BY TRACEY ROWLAND

WORD on FIRE
ACADEMIC

Published by Word on Fire Academic, an imprint of Word on Fire,
Elk Grove Village, IL 60007
© 2025 by Word on Fire Catholic Ministries
Printed in the United States of America
All rights reserved

Cover design, typesetting, and interior art direction by Megan Travers, Nicolas
Fredrickson, Clark Kenyon, and Rozann Lee.

Scripture excerpts are from the Revised Standard Version
Bible: Catholic Edition (copyright © 1966), used by permission of the
National Council of the Churches of Christ in the United States of America.
All rights reserved worldwide.

No part of this book may be used or reproduced in any manner whatsoever
without written permission, except in the case of brief quotations in critical
articles or reviews. For more information, contact Word on Fire Catholic
Ministries, PO Box 97330, Washington, DC 20090-7330 or email
contact@wordonfire.org.

First printing, April 2025

ISBN: 978-1-68578-139-2

Library of Congress Control Number: 2024937321

Contents

Translator's Acknowledgments

Translating Erich Przywara is notoriously difficult, and several people helped make this translation of Przywara's *Kant Today* possible. First, I extend my thanks to John R. Betz, Reinhard Hütter, Travis Lacy, and Sebastian Condon for their invaluable contributions, including insights on numerous technical terms unique to continental philosophy. Jason C. Paone also helped polish the Greek and Latin. In addition, I am deeply grateful to my wife, Esther, for her unwavering support and patience during the many hours spent grappling with the complexities of Przywara's idiosyncratic prose (a frequent topic of our dinner conversations). Lastly, I want to thank my son Joseph Martin. Although he did not contribute to the translation per se, he adds value to everything I do.

Introduction

Erich Przywara, SJ (1889–1972), was one of the great names in German Catholic scholarship of the twentieth century. From 1922 until 1941, he worked in the editorial office of the journal *Stimmen der Zeit*, for which he produced 120 essays. His complete bibliography amounted to over eight hundred titles, including fifty books. He was a mentor to Edith Stein (St. Teresa Benedicta of the Cross), Hans Urs von Balthasar, Karl Rahner, and Josef Pieper, among many others. Balthasar described him as "the greatest spirit I was ever permitted to meet."[1] Pieper said that in the interwar years in Germany, there was hardly "anyone as thoroughly at home in the great tradition of philosophy and theology (and not only of the European tradition) as Erich Przywara."[2] Moreover, "it was the public disputation between him and Karl Barth, which took place at the University of Münster . . . that started the 'dialogue' between the Christian denominations."[3] The key issue in the debate with Barth was Przywara's concept of the *analogia entis*, famously described by Barth as the "invention of the anti-Christ."[4] Przywara's magnum opus—*Analogia Entis* (1932)—was published two years after *Kant Today*'s appearance in 1930.[5]

1. Hans Urs von Balthasar, *My Work: In Retrospect* (San Francisco: Ignatius, 1993), 89.

2. Josef Pieper, *No One Could Have Known: An Autobiography: The Early Years, 1904–1945*, trans. Graham Harrison (San Francisco: Ignatius, 1987), 66. Originally published as *Noch wußte es niemand: Autobiographische Aufzeichnungen 1904–1945* (Munich, DE: Kösel-Verlag, 1976).

3. Pieper, 67.

4. For an extensive analysis of this concept and the debates it engendered, see *Analogy of Being: Invention of the Anti-Christ or Wisdom of God?*, ed. Thomas Joseph White (Grand Rapids, MI: Eerdmans, 2010).

5. For the English translation of *Analogia Entis*, with an introduction by John R. Betz, see *Analogia Entis: Metaphysics: Original Structure and Universal Rhythm*, trans. John R. Betz and David Bentley Hart (Grand Rapids, MI: Eerdmans, 2013). See also John R. Betz, "The *Analogia Entis* as a Standard of Catholic Engagement: Erich Przywara's Critique of Phenomenology and Dialectical Theology," *Modern Theology* 35, no. 1 (January 2019): 81–102; Francesca Aran Murphy, "The Sound of the *Analogia Entis*: Part I," *New Blackfriars* 74, no. 876 (November

Another major and related issue in the interwar period was what to make of the legacy of German idealism, and this issue is the subject of *Kant Today*. As Holger Zaborowski noted, after the First World War, the "narratives of the Enlightenment tradition, of progress, reason, science, and freedom, became deeply questionable."[6] The theologian Paul Tillich recalled an experience from the front in World War I. He said, "All that horrible, long night I walked along the rows of dying men, and much of my German classical education broke down that night."[7] The Polish historian of Marxism Leszek Kołakowski described the "recurrent German philosophical desire," for which Kant is the standard-bearer, as that of the attempt to "discover God without God, to find a secular and transcendental foundation for moral and epistemological security apart from God."[8] Hans Urs von Balthasar summarized the moves on the intellectual chessboard by saying that "Luther deposes Aristotelian reason in order to make room for faith, but this rejected reason acquires a Cartesian structure and Kant tries to tame it by bringing it under human control. Being thus limited, reason no longer has anything to do with religion and it becomes what Karl Barth called an 'idol factory.'"[9]

1993): 508–21; and Francesca Aran Murphy, "The Sound of the *Analogia Entis*: Part II," *New Blackfriars* 74, no. 877 (December 1993): 557–65. For reviews of *Kant Today*, see Nozza Libano, review of *Kant Heute*, by Erich Przywara, *Rivista di Filosofia Neo-Scolastica* 23, no. 4/5 (1931): 465–68, and Georg Siegmund, review of *Kant Heute*, by Erich Przywara, *Philosophisches Jahrbuch* 44 (1931): 255–56.

6. Holger Zaborowski, "Contradiction, Liturgy, and Freedom: Romano Guardini's Search for Meaning after the Cataclysm of World War I," *Modern Theology* 35, no. 1 (January 2019): 43–54, at 44.

7. Paul Tillich, *Time*, March 16, 1959, 47. Quoted in Douglas John Hall, "'The Great War' and the Theologians," in *The Twentieth Century: A Theological Overview*, ed. Gregory Baum (Maryknoll, NY: Orbis, 1999), 3–14, at 6.

8. Leszek Kołakowski, "Reprodukcja kulturalna i zapominanie," in *Czy diabeł może być zbawiony i 27 innych kazań* (Kraków, PL: Znak, 2006), 80. Quoted in Artur Mrówczyński-Van Allen, *Between the Icon and the Idol: The Human Person and the Modern State in Russian Literature and Thought—Chaadayev, Soloviev, Grossman*, trans. Matthew Philipp Whelan (Eugene, OR: Cascade, 2013), 130.

9. Hans Urs von Balthasar, *Love Alone Is Credible*, trans. D.C. Schindler (San Francisco: Ignatius, 2004), 16. For a more extensive account of the situation of German idealism after

Przywara shared Barth's opposition to the idol factory, and his *Kant Today* situates Kant within a genealogy that extends all the way back to Parmenides and Heraclitus on the one side and down to the idol factory on the other. The work is presented in four sections. The first is a historical overview of recurring polarities in philosophical thought. If the doctrine of the *analogia entis* is the single most important doctrine in Przywara's framework (embracing the disciplines of philosophy and theology), the concept of "polarity" is the single most important key to understanding his methodology.[10] Przywara's publications almost always take the form of explorations of polarities, and *Kant Today* is typical of this form. Przywara's essays have a seesawing quality—first tracing one end of an intellectual pole and then examining the opposite end of the pole before attending to the issue of how they have been or might be synthesized. Thus, in the first section of *Kant Today*, Przywara highlights the polarities between Parmenides, who holds the flag for the eternal transcendent world of ideas floating above history, and Heraclitus, who is the champion of the idea of constant flux within history. The polar tension between these two philosophers morphs into the polar tension between Plato and Aristotle. With the arrival of Christianity, a new polarity emerges between the Johannine presentation of Christ as the Logos and the Pauline presentation of Christ as the great stumbling block to all earthly wisdom in the First Letter to the Corinthians. This is followed within the thought of St. Augustine with a further polarity between "Deus-Veritas" and "Deus-Caritas"—God as truth and God as love. All of these polarities then find a resolution of their tension in the synthesis of St. Thomas, where one can see "Parmenides interwoven with Heraclitus, Plato agleam in

World War I, see Tracey Rowland, *Beyond Kant and Nietzsche: The Munich Defence of Christian Humanism* (London: Bloomsbury, 2021), 5–9.

10. For an understanding of how this concept works in Przywara's thought, see Erich Przywara, *Polarity: A German Catholic's Interpretation of Religion*, trans. A.C. Bouquet (Oxford: Oxford University Press, 1935).

Aristotle, the Johannine Logos revealed in Pauline Agape," and thus, "the divine All of an idea-illuminating, living Love" (8). This brilliant synthesis, however, is perhaps so taut that it quickly "wobbles," and there emerges the contrast between late-Scholastic Thomism and Scotism. The dichotomy becomes one of a choice for Parmenides over Heraclitus, for the Johannine Logos over the Pauline Agape (baroque Thomism), or Heraclitus over Parmenides, Pauline Agape over the Johannine Logos (Scotism). Notwithstanding this choice, both Thomists and Scotists affirm the *analogia entis*. The stage is now set for the drama of the Reformation, out of which there emerges both a rationalist absolutism and the irrationalism of the pure faith of experience—both extremes cutting themselves loose from the *analogia entis*. When Kant tries to rebuild a synthesis, he eschews all recourse to the *analogia entis* doctrine, God is "practically confined" within the creature, and the creature's quest to partake in the divine nature by its receptivity to divine illumination and its practice of the theological virtue of love is replaced by an "abrupt storm, raging back-and-forth," of a titanic desire to be like God, to possess God-like powers (13). We have arrived at the point identified by Kołakowski as the recurrent German temptation.

The second section of *Kant Today* then offers a detailed account of the different intellectual choices taken by St. Thomas and Kant, marshaled under their responses to three foundational issues in philosophy, which Przywara calls the problem of validity, the problem of reality, and the problem of individuality. Przywara argues that in stark contrast to Kant, St. Thomas does not attempt to solve the problem of validity within man but rather leaves the issue wide open. The problem, so to speak, is part of the human condition itself, which is to be a creature, not a creator. Przywara declares that if men "claim the omnipotence and fullness of God for themselves, the result is not an 'Absolute' but rather its caricature: the 'Extreme'" (37). It is for this reason that Przywara's key insight is sometimes summarized by the idea that if you reject the *analogia entis* (as Kant did), you end up in a gulag.

On the subject of gulags, one of the unexpected gems in this section is Przywara's discussion of socialism. While Kant is often regarded as a significant figure in the tradition of liberalism, Przywara makes the case for his paternity of the socialist movement. Przywara explains how the oppositions between "communal universalism (where the individual is regarded as a passive offshoot of the universal)" and "anti-communal individualism (where everything universal is at the mercy of the individual's whims)" (40) are merely alternative outcomes of the contradictions within the Kantian synthesis itself.

Significantly, in his analysis of Aquinas, Przywara argues that St. Thomas should not be understood as a "Christian Aristotelian" but rather as someone who occupied a position between the "dogmatism" of early Augustinian—and thus, Neoplatonic—thought and the "critical" philosophy of the Aristotelianism taught at the Sorbonne in his age (45). This contrast between dogmatism and criticism is one of the many polarities highlighted by Przywara. An emphasis on criticism gives rise to a critical epistemological theory, while an emphasis on dogmatism gives rise to a metaphysics of the spiritual. A key similarity between St. Thomas and Kant, according to Przywara, is their mutual search for a synthesis of these positions. Notwithstanding this similarity, the two end up with radically different syntheses because of the difference between Catholic Christianity and Lutheran Christianity. For Przywara, there is a Lutheran undertow in Kantian anthropology, however much Kant tries to escape the influence of theology upon philosophy. Przywara believes that Lutheran Christianity gave birth to two spiritual trajectories that cannot be reconciled. There is, first, the position of "God alone," which entails a rejection of the *analogia entis*, with the result that all of creation, including the human intellect, is utterly fallen and reason behaves like a "whore" (52) And second, there is the position of "Deus in nobis" or "God in us," which reduces God to something like the "divine luster of . . . 'pure reason'" (52). In contrast, in Thomistic anthropology, infused with a Catholic spirituality, God and the human person are connected by the *analogia entis* such that human free will, though wounded by the fall and hampered by concupiscence, can still, with grace, pursue the good discerned by the intellect to be true. This means the faculties of the soul (including the intellect and will) can still work in perfect freedom and harmony.

The third section offers an examination of the neo-Kantian schools of the interwar period and Catholic engagements with the thought of Kant, in particular the contribution of the Belgian Jesuit Joseph Maréchal (1878–1944), who is popularly regarded as the father of transcendental Thomism. In this third section of the work, Przywara also traces the treatment of issues in Kantian metaphysics by Martin Heidegger (1889–1976) and Eugen Herrigel (1884–1955). Both early-twentieth-century German philosophers had an interest in Buddhism and the relationship between mysticism and German idealism. Herrigel lived in Japan from 1924–1929 and was influenced by Zen Buddhism.[11] He is not well known today, perhaps because, like Heidegger, his work is tainted by an association with the Nazi movement.[12] Przywara reads Heidegger and Herrigel as offering two different responses to the Kantian question "How are synthetic a priori judgments possible?" Heidegger offers what Przywara calls a "metaphysics of finitude," while Herrigel offers what he calls a "metaphysics of infinity." Przywara argues that the only alternative to these either/or options is the *analogia entis*.

---

11. Samuel Baudinette, "Meister Eckhart, Eugen Herrigel and the European Reading of Japanese Budō," Academia, January 2023, https://www.academia.edu/8572796/Meister_Eckhart_Eugen_Herrigel_and_the_European_Reading_of_Japanese_Budo.

12. Though even more so than Heidegger: when Herrigel returned to Germany from Japan, he became a member of the Militant League for German Culture, a pro-Nazi organization.

In the fourth and shortest section of *Kant Today*, Przywara recommends the thought of St. John Henry Newman as the best contemporary effort to rebuild a synthesis, especially Newman's ideas about explicit and implicit reason outlined in the *Essay in Aid of a Grammar of Assent*.[13] He describes Newman's achievement as the offering of Thomist wisdom in the language of Augustine. He noted that Newman had to contend with both rationalism and empiricism in epistemology and with rationalism and sentimentalism in fundamental theology. Przywara describes the primary trait of Newman's worldview as the idea of the mutable world and mutable man held within the immutability of God—the *analogia entis* thereby surfaces again.

Przywara's *Kant Today* is therefore a typical example of German Catholic intellectual life in the interwar years insofar as it is an engagement with German idealism and what had become of this tradition for scholars who wrote after the trauma of the First World War. Its message is that Newman, not Heidegger or Herrigel or Kant or the neo-Kantians, offers a way out of the cul-de-sac in which European philosophy found itself once it abandoned the Thomistic *analogia entis*. The juxtaposition of Heidegger and Herrigel was prescient insofar as the generation of 1968 would despair of the European philosophical tradition and go in search of other approaches to self-transcendence in the mystical traditions of the Far East. Yoga would replace Eucharistic Adoration. Przywara, one of those German national heroes who offered intellectual resistance to Hitler and his peculiar version of neo-paganism, had a better idea. The translation of *Kant Today* into English now makes the Przywara alternative accessible to a new generation of Catholic scholars almost a century after

13. John Henry Newman, *An Essay in Aid of a Grammar of Assent* (n.p.: Assumption Press, 2013). See also the essays by Michael Dauphinais and Michael Pakaluk in *A Guide to John Henry Newman: His Life and Thought*, ed. Juan R. Vélez (Washington, DC: The Catholic University of America Press, 2022).

Kant Today first appeared in the twilight years of the doomed Weimar Republic.

Tracey Rowland
Mont Albert, January 20, 2023

Preface

The title *Kant Today* says, in general, that this work is not about a particular interpretation of Kant but about engaging the vitality of his thought 'today.' This 'today' can, in one sense, be understood from our own personal perspective. Taken this way, it refers to the 'today' of certain philosophical tendencies. In this respect, this work has a philosophical-historical purpose: to situate the inner encounter between Kant and Thomas Aquinas in today's philosophical crises and revolutions. Equally, however, this work is also about an objective 'today': it is concerned with the problem of a metaphysics of the *analogia entis*, which arises out of all problems.

This brings us to the methodology of these elucidations. They each translate a personal-historical situation into a stage within the objective history of the problem and flow from there into a pure, objective philosophy.[1] The author is indebted to Georg Simmel for this methodology, as he owes thanks to Edmund Husserl for the objective analysis. In both methodology and analysis, Augustine and Thomas are his living masters.

This is a 'survey,' as stated in the title, because this work is not intended as a meticulous individual study; rather, its purpose is a mediation of views arising from living philosophical controversies.

The author has presented the thoughts contained in these studies multiple times in lectures in recent years in Worms, Basel, Trier, Zürich, and Freiburg. The engagement with Maréchal first appeared in extended form as a critique in the *Philosophisches Jahrbuch*, 1928.

Munich, Easter 1930.

1. *sachlichen Problemsgeschichte . . . Sach-Philosophie.* Przywara uses terms like *sachlich* and *Sache* in contrast to subjective philosophies (that begin with consciousness) to refer to philosophies that begin with the 'object.'—Trans.

1

Historical Perspectives

PARMENIDES–HERACLITUS; JOHN–PAUL; AUGUSTINE

Two great philosophical orientations confront each other at the
dawn of European philosophy, one as the heir of Eastern wisdom
and lifestyle, the other containing the seed of the coming primacy
of the West. On the one hand, we have the strict philosophy of
Parmenides, a philosophy of the timeless, transcendent world of
ideas above the grand illusion of becoming, a philosophical orientation that foregrounds unity's changeless, eternal being. On
the other hand, we have the *Panta rhei*, Heraclitus's "Everything
is flux," the philosophy of the perpetual, creative impulse, multiplicity's eternal becoming, whose abiding rhythm is but eternal
movement. On the one side, then, we have such an emphasis on
the eternal hierarchy of eternal ideas[1] that life becomes frozen
within it. On the other side, we have such an emphasis on the
eternity of living movement that the ideas dissolve into its formal rhythm.

It is true that the era of Plato and Aristotle tried to bring
about an inner reconciliation of this antithesis[2]. Plato binds the
nonbeing of becoming and the true being of the ideal-eternal together in the unified form of the former's 'participation' in the
latter, and, to an increasing degree (from the ecstasy of youth to
the prudence of age), the ideal world of being sinks into the heart
of the sensory world of becoming. Aristotle, in turn, leads this

1. *Inhalte.*—Trans.
2. *Gegensatz.*—Trans.

inner-Platonic process to its conclusion—to the resolution of the ideas into the principles of movement that structure the process of becoming itself, but such that the world of becoming thereby shifts from a whirl of movement into a sort of world of ideas made visible, into a cosmos comprised by grades of being.

And yet, doesn't the inner methodology of these two great synthetic systems already demonstrate that the two great antitheses of Parmenides and Heraclitus have only been refined therein but not yet overcome? For doesn't Plato vacillate between an (early) philosophy, where the meaning[3] of becoming is—in virtue of 'participation'—to merge into the being of the idea, and a (late) philosophy where the substantial world of ideas almost acquires the meaning of being rendered visible into the world of becoming: between redemption[4] into being and dissolution[5] into becoming? And doesn't Aristotle offer an (early) philosophy that, when pressed to its logical conclusion, leads to the dissolution of the 'rigid *eidē*' into fluid becoming? And doesn't his (late) philosophy, in turn, see the meaning of becoming in a structure of being in which it is both immanent and absent? Thus, doesn't his philosophy swing back from dissolution into becoming to redemption into being? In the process, doesn't the sliding tension between Heraclitus and Parmenides simply become a law within these supposed syntheses, a law of tension that simply jostles back and forth[6]?

A pair of similar orientations also appear to stand at the outset of Christianity. According to the concluding verse of the prologue to the Gospel of John and the familiar phrase of the Second Letter to the Corinthians (4:6), Christ the Lord is the "proclamation" of God, "whom no one has ever seen" (John 1:18), in whose "face" God "has shone" (2 Cor. 4:6). The dim grasping

3. *Sinn.*—Trans.
4. *Erlösung.*—Trans.
5. *Entlösung.*—Trans.
6. *inneren Spannungsgesetz des Auf und Nieder.*—Trans.

of philosophy after the 'origin and end of things' (as the ancient Ionian philosophers characterized the task of philosophy), this groping of the "people who sat in darkness" and the "shadow of death" is overshone by a "great light" (Matt. 4:16). For the 'origin himself' speaks. Yet this is the final, ineluctable veiling, for even this self-revelation "in the face of Jesus Christ," as Thomas Aquinas puts it, also speaks to us but "in signis creatis," in creaturely signs and so also in their dichotomies.[7] The fabric and history of the world is permeated by the "great light" that shines in Christ as the "light of the world," yet [still] within the "mirrors of creatures." Thus, within Scripture itself, two views of the world, illumined by God in Christ, are contrasted.

For John, Christ is the Logos who enters the world. He is the transcendent, shining truth of ideas become the reality of flesh. Through him, the consecration of God comes upon a groping philosophical conception that views the [physical] world as the birth of the radiant world of ideas in the gleam of unchanging, timeless truth. For the Apostle to the Gentiles in the First Letter to the Corinthians, however, Christ is the great contradiction[8] to the luminous ideas of philosophical wisdom, the rupture within their well-constructed trains of thought. Christ is also a birth, but the birth of the incomprehensibility of the living God, whose freedom shatters all clever conceptual necessities. From him, a divine consecration comes over a probing line of human inquiry, which—at times wearily, at times bitterly, at times gently smiling—shakes its head at all well-constructed systems, which are torn apart by the uncontainable surge of flowing life. This orientation places the love of shared life and understanding (*agape*) over an all-encompassing knowledge (*gnosis*).

So, Christian thinkers have been presented with a more challenging task: to reveal the center that unites the two orientations.

7. Thomas Aquinas, *Super Boetium de Trinitate* 2.6.3.
8. *Widerspruch.*—Trans.

The unity is given by God, but the current of life is ever inclined, time and again, to rush straight through one or the other of the two ways. The middle way is illuminated from the outset but repeatedly traversed anew through the recurring darkness of the extremes.

In *Augustine*, the task of finding the middle way is inscribed as the decisive problem for times to come. On the one hand, he is undeniably the Church doctor of *Deus-Veritas*, God-Truth, and therein, the Christian culmination of a development that passed over from the speculative ideas of the Greeks into the Platonic theological thought of the Alexandrian school—from the divinity of the Logos of ideas into the theology of the God-Logos. On the other hand, he is no less the vigorous advocate of the living primal force of love against its contemplative dissolution (*anapausis*—repose) by the Alexandrians. Departing from the Alexandrians, another confession of God awakens in him: the confession of *Deus-Caritas*, God-Love, and of the ultimate incomprehensibility of a love surpassing knowledge. Thus, his unified word for God is 'Deus Lux Caritas,' God as Light-Love: 'Light' being the Neo-platonic word for the all-pervasive power of truth, and 'Love' the word for a primacy of life over understanding. The soul's unified stance toward God (in this unified conception)[9] is expressed as "quiescendo operari et operando quiescere."[10] *Quiescere* ("rest") is the attitude of contemplation toward the pure ideas, and *operari* ("work") is the word for the active restlessness of caring love. Still, in Augustine, there is a final, unresolved back-and-forth between the two orientations that he tries to keep in check. At times, it seems as if active love completely loses itself in world-surpassing bliss in the contemplation of pure truth; at other times, it seems as if its fine sense for life's incomprehensibility triumphs over the clear vision of eternal order. Augustine embodies the inner

9. *die Einheitshaltung der Seele zu diesem Einheits-Göttlichen.*—Trans.
10. resting work and working rest.—Trans.

vitality of our problem, the vitality of a struggle that plays out in times to come.

II

THOMAS AQUINAS AND KANT

Beyond its vital form, the problem has been given a theoretical solution in two central personalities: Thomas Aquinas and Immanuel Kant.

What *Thomas Aquinas* faced in opposing directions is called (in the history of philosophy) the Platonic Augustinianism of early Scholasticism and the Aristotelianism of the Parisian Arts Faculty. They are, as the names suggest, philosophical inclinations, one of which accentuates the Platonic contemplative beholding of ideas and, in them, the 'eternal world' of pure, essential order, while the other is borne by the Aristotelian pathos for self-contained movement and believes in the 'world of becoming' in the flow of time. The particular shortcoming[11] of these inclinations is that they both ultimately attempt to derive philosophy from theology—that in them, a certain theology forges its own intrinsic philosophy. The "Credo ut intelligam" or "Fides quaerens intellectum"[12] of Anselm of Canterbury, the great master of the Scholastic method, is common to both. Still, they are theologies with different accents. The theology of Platonic Augustinianism is the theology of the luminous, ideal *Deus-Veritas*[13]; its symbolic imagery is the world of ideal, pure essences. The theology of the neo-Aristotelianism of the Arts Faculty, however, believes in a God of infinite vitality. As a result, it is the man of undiminished vitality that is interiorly closest to God—not the man who contemplates eternal order but the man who strives for the infinite;

---

11. *Stigma.*—Trans.
12. 'I believe that I may understand' or 'Faith seeking understanding.'—Trans.
13. *Idee-hellen Deus-Veritas.*—Trans.

not the calm systematizer but the searching aporetic[14]; not the man of 'being' but the man of 'becoming.'

Now, the history of philosophy identifies Thomas as an Aristotelian who tried to synthesize Augustinianism and Aristotelianism. But what does this mean for our question? The first answer is provided by his teaching on God at the outset of his great *Summa*. This teaching is synthetic, to be sure. For it replaces the Augustinian concept of 'participation' with the concept of 'causality,' and it recasts the Aristotelian argument from 'motion' so that God does not appear as the unmoved mover 'for' the motion—that is, causally external to it—but rather 'above' the motion as its transcendent, self-sufficient primary cause. But the 'way' to God *ex motu* (from motion) nevertheless remains (and has remained in the Thomistic schools) the formative 'way.'

Thomas emphatically believes in the 'living' God of the 'living' world. This is clearly shown in how he understands this world in terms of (subjective) knowing and (objective) being. The world in its being fundamentally does not present itself to a purely contemplative knowing, to the intuitive understanding of ideas; rather, the world's truth formally flashes forth in the energetic knowing of the *intellectus agens*, "active thinking," and in the intellect's act of *dividere et componere*—i.e., in its analyzing and synthesizing activity. Accordingly, the world in its being is neither a static realm of pure essence[15] nor one of absolute motion. Rather, it is the moving unity-in-tension[16] of abiding essence in moved existence. Nor again does the world consist of a pure, existing essence or of essence as a pure, fleeting expression of self-contained existence in its sheer flux; rather, it is the tension of essence toward existence, of essence beyond and in becoming—of essence in-and-beyond[17] existence. The world, as such, is

14. *nicht der besitzruhige Systematiker, sondern der suchende Aporetiker.*—Trans.

15. *eine ruhende Bildwelt reinen Soseins.*—Trans.

16. *Bewegungs-Spannungs-Eins.*—Trans.

17. *in-über.*—Trans.

a duality: On the one hand, it is a moving tension of becoming in a sense that stresses the creature as always *in potentia*, in a state of becoming, in contrast to God as sheer *actus*, the becoming-less *Is*. But on the other hand, the world is a properly causal[18] tension of becoming—i.e., not (as pure Aristotelianism would have it) as the inner *in potentia* to the divine *actus* but rather as a relatively autonomous[19] 'actus in potentia,' causally effective in itself, the *causa secunda*.

By virtue of this inner correlation between autonomous creaturely knowing and autonomous creaturely being, however, the 'living' God now logically shifts into a tensed[20], transcendent height above the 'living' world. For since neither creaturely knowing nor creaturely being are His non-substantial appearance[21], so too their movement toward Him is not an encompassing and comprehending possession of His nearness and comprehensibility. Rather, as Thomas shows in his commentary on Boethius's *De Trinitate*, for the creature who approaches, God surpasses similarity with creaturely substances into a tensed dissimilarity and separation from them, shifting from *Deus notus* to *Deus tamquam ignotus*,[22] the 'unknown God' of incomprehensibility. Consequently, the movement of the creature toward Him becomes a tensed *in potentia*—a becoming toward infinity.

Thus, Thomas's thought is characterized by two aspects. On the one hand, there is a clear order of creaturely grades of being and a clear subordination of creatures under God. On the other, there is an inner-creaturely order that consistently leads back to the irresolvable, mysterious tension[23] of the 'actus in potentia,' an order between creatures and God that speaks to the continuous

---

18. *eigenwirksame.*—Trans.
19. *eigenständigeigenwirksamer.*—Trans.
20. *betonte.*—Trans.
21. *wesenlose Erscheinung.*—Trans.
22. the known God to God as unknown.—Trans.
23. *Spannungsgeheimnis.*—Trans.

upward stretching of a creature moving toward God—from the *Deus notus* of comprehensibility in symbols to the *Deus tamquam ignotus* beyond symbols. There is a harmony [in Thomas's thought], but one that, by virtue of its ultimate mystery, is in motion, a unity in rhythm, Parmenides interwoven with Heraclitus, Plato agleam in Aristotle, the Johannine Logos revealed in Pauline Agape: the divine All of an idea-illuminating, living Love.

Yet, it is the fate of man-made unities that the masters meet their end in their disciples' quarrels. In Thomas, a genuine, contemplative Augustinianism that stresses placid understanding is still bound together with an Aristotelianism that delights in activity and underscores a dynamic seeking and striving. For although, in Thomas, the will appears as a direct effect of knowing, still, this knowing contains something of a unity of knowing and willing by virtue of its intensely energetic character. Yet the two schools that are sharply opposed after the death of Aquinas—Thomism and Scotism—divide the unity between them. In Thomism, given its doctrines of the direct knowledge of universal essences, individuals as the quantification of the universal (*individuum de ratione materiae*), and the real severance (not merely real *difference* or *tension*)[24] between eternal essence and moved existence—given such overemphasis therein on placid eternal unity over against the dynamism of a universe of real individuals—the world becomes essentially another eternal, shimmering Augustinian image-world of venerable contemplation. They opted for Parmenides over Heraclitus, the Johannine Logos over Pauline Agape.

In Scotism, on the other hand, the doctrine of the real identity of essence and existence, coupled with an emphasis on the formal character of thought, and finally, the fundamental primacy of will over intellect—with the autonomy it entails of a freedom founded on itself—lead to a picture of God and the

---

24. *Realgeschiedenheit (nicht nur Realverschiedenheit oder Real-Spannung).*—Trans.

world[25] in which the life of the world is incomprehensibly moved by the incomprehensible vitality of God's absolute freedom: vital movement for its own sake. They opted for Heraclitus over Parmenides, for the knowledge-surpassing Pauline Agape over the Johannine Logos. Formed unity (in Thomism) stands against concentrated infinity (in Scotism).

Thomism and Scotism, despite their sharp differences, are united by their shared commitment to the ontological *analogia entis*: God is all but not all alone, and for that reason the creature has 'its very self from God'[26] but is not merely His non-substantial appearing. Thus, a background unity buttresses a foreground diversity. Yet it was the disastrous fate of late Scholasticism that this bulwark began to falter until it collapsed in the Reformation amidst Luther's doctrine of mono-causality[27]. On one side, there arose (in the meanderings of nominalism) such an exaggeration of the autonomy of reason that it availed itself of the right to judge matters of faith. From a relative primacy of knowledge (still subordinate to God) emerged the absolutism of rationalism. However, on the other side (in the meanderings of voluntarist late Scotism), the factor of God's incomprehensible vital freedom toward the world was exaggerated to such an extent that all established truth—philosophical as well as theological— dissolved into the functionalism of an incomprehensible, purely factual blind will of 'sic jubeo' [thus I command] and 'so it pleases me'! From a relative primacy of the freedom of the will emerged the absolutism of irrationalism. With this, the decisive position of the Reformation was already internally prepared.

For in the Reformation, two tendencies intersect. [1] The first tendency—in the extreme realization of the irrationalism of late Scotism—traces all matters[28] back to the irrational

---

25. *Gottes-Welt-Bild.*—Trans.
26. *Eigen von Gott her.*—Trans.
27. *Alleinwirksamkeitslehre.*—Trans.
28. *Inhalt.*—Trans.

act-experience[29] that is alone divine, reducing the objectivity of faith to the sheer state of belief: in the irrational bestowal of damnation and grace[30], God is humanity's sole and total truth. Yet precisely by virtue of the fact that this doctrine elevates the individual, God-experiencing subject, who is supported by the insight of such an experience against the received theology of the Church (which demands the subjection of all insight), this direction, in the irrationalism of the sheer state of belief, already provides the impetus that, in the following centuries, will transform the totality of the God who provides certainty of salvation into the totality of divinized human reason[31]. If the first direction carries such a conception of the unity of man and God[32] as its ultimate formal principle—wherein everything creaturely dissolves into the (theopanistic) irrationality of God's mono-causality (comprised of judgment and mercy[33])—then [2] the unity of man and God conceived of in the second direction is one in which God (who is transcendent over all insight) merges into the divinized insight of 'pure humanity's' reason. Thus, from a religious root, there arises the starkest pair of antitheses that cuts right through modernity from here on out: [a] the experiential irrationalism that culminates in the denial of established truth in general, and [b] the rationalism (deriving everything from first principles) that culminates in an idealism that dissolves reality altogether.

From this vantage point, having surveyed [1] the exaggeration of the antithesis between Thomism and Scotism (which was, however, subdued by their agreement on the *analogia entis*), having passed on from there to [2] the ruptured antithesis between nominalism and late Scotism, and on through [3] the irreparable rift between rationalism and irrationalism in the Reformation,

29. *Akt-Erlebens.*—Trans.
30. *Verdammung-Begnadung.*—Trans.
31. *göttlicher Vernunft-Humanität.*—Trans.
32. *Gott-Mensch-Eins.*—Trans.
33. *Gericht-Barmherzigkeit.*—Trans.

and having then arrived at [4] the contradictory chaos between modernity's a-rational empiricism and a priori rationalism—from this vantage point, we are now in a position where we can turn our gaze to [5] the second attempt at unification—Kant.

We are accustomed to viewing *Kant*'s decisive standpoint—what he calls his 'Copernican revolution'—as a shift from an orientation of man to the world (where his knowledge receives its laws from the world) to an orienting of the world by man (where human reason gives its laws to nature). This is, of course, not to be understood first in the sense of an anthropocentric stratification of the world around man as its center. For Kant could not otherwise first speak of a 'Copernican revolution,' which precisely—in contrast to the Ptolemaic centering of the cosmos around the earth of man—sought to understand this earth as but a part alongside other parts in the overarching entirety of the cosmos. But it also does not align with the emphatically skeptical or at least critically limiting sense of Kant's 'man as the lawgiver of nature,' which affirms a world shaped by humans since he denies we can apprehend the world 'in itself.' On the other hand, as both [1] the *Lectures on Metaphysics* and [2] the sense of the progression from the pure critique in the *Critique of Pure Reason* to the attempted synthesis in the *Critique of Judgment* seem to clarify, the customary sense of 'man as the lawgiver of nature' persists (and even intensifies). For Kant, not only does the 'real world' increasingly become a formal unity between the 'sensory world' as matter and the 'intelligible world' as form, but the deeper foundation of the skepticism apparent earlier is developed too: the doctrine of human receptivity as the internal limitation, containment, and attenuation of the inherently divine spontaneity (*Deus in nobis!*) of pure thinking. Thinking, conceived of as pure spontaneity, is creative of things[34]. It recognizes the 'things in themselves' because and insofar as they are its creation. Yet this spontaneity of man's

34. *ding-schöpferisch.*—Trans.

intellectus archetypus is completely saturated in receptivity, and so the original 'lawgiver of nature' in man simultaneously implies the abovementioned delimitation and denial.

Thus, we gain a clear view of the true meaning of Kant's solution. Confronted with the sundered extremes of [1] an empiricism that denies the spontaneity of thinking and asserts only receptivity, and [2] a rationalism that only knows spontaneity, Kant aims at a unity of the two, just as Thomas did earlier. But between Thomas and Kant lies the fatal dissolution of the God-creature relationship of the *analogia entis* in the Reformation's [doctrine of divine] mono-causality. Thus, unlike in the case of Thomas, the inner tension between spontaneity and receptivity in human thinking does not point beyond itself[35] to God's sole spontaneity; rather, the spontaneity in man is the Divine itself. The inner tension between spontaneity and receptivity is the tension between God and creature in the one human being. However, from out of *this* tension that resolves harmoniously, there arises the sundered, unbridgeable antithesis between the Alone-Holy and the ever-sinful[36] (as the doctrine of mono-causality between God and creature demands).

The typical Kantian doctrine of 'infinite progress' arises from this. The divine in the individual human is the 'transcendental subject' or the 'transcendental ideal,' toward which the 'empirical subject' is always striving without ever being able to reach it, indeed without being allowed to, for it is on this unbridgeable antithesis, as Arthur Liebert puts it, that the essence of the 'transcendental subject' depends—namely, its ideal antithesis to the empirical. Thus, the unity of spontaneity and receptivity becomes a tragic contradiction in man himself. They are supposed to be one, but their unity consists in their sharpest distance. This distance increases even more when we pass over from thinking

35. *Übersich-hinaus-weisen.*—Trans.
36. *Allein-Heiligen . . . Immer-Sünder.*—Trans.

to willing and, from there, to our fundamental dispositions[37]. For in willing, spontaneity becomes the absolute autonomy of the transcendental character, while receptivity intensifies into the empirical will's complete bondage to duty. Spontaneity rises to that sovereign height of the entirely groundless, self-empowered freedom resting in itself, ascribed to God by Ockham, while receptivity now explicitly takes on the traits of the Lutheran sinner's will, which is only ever 'driven.' Thus arises that frightful contradiction that gapes in the deepest depths of the Kantian man: the Olympian 'divine humanity' and the inextirpable 'radical evil'— God and the devil as one man.

For Thomas, God stands beyond man, and therefore, secure in his orientation toward Him, man oscillates between receiving and doing as the two inherently positive sides of his created nature, now internally resolved[38]. For Kant, God is confined within humanity as the 'Humanity-God'[39], *Deus in nobis*, and therefore, the oscillation between receiving and doing must tear apart into the distinctively Lutheran antithesis of 'judgment,' the judgment of unapproachable divinity over the creature aspiring to be God[40], the damning judgment of 'God alone' over a creature who is inherently, originally sinful. It is a unity, but an irredeemably tragic one. Indeed, as with Thomas, it is a unity of accentuated movement since, in Kant, the 'infinite progress' corresponds to the 'actus in potentia' or 'motus' or 'appetitus naturalis' in Aquinas. However, with Kant, because God, considered as the limiting idea of this movement, is practically confined to the realm of the created, it is not, as with Thomas, a harmonious movement in which the transcendent vitality of God's infinite life reveals itself—God, whose eternally living likeness is found in the creature's temporal vitality. Instead, it is the abrupt storm, raging back-and-forth in

37. *letzten Einstellungen.*—Trans.
38. *geloste.*—Trans.
39. *Humanität-Gott.*—Trans.
40. *Gott-sein-wollende-Geschöpflichkeit.*—Trans.

a constant ascent and descent of wanting to be god-like. It is not the hymn of the servant's liberation but the tragedy of the titan.

2

Kant and Thomas

KANT'S INNER ANTITHESIS

There are three fundamental problems that occupy Kant's thought, but they also generally form the backbone of all philosophy:

[1] the problem of validity,
[2] the problem of reality, and
[3] the problem of individuality.

The first question the inquiring human mind asks is: Is there, among the great flow of opinions, an absolute truth? This question discloses the problem of validity—i.e., valid truth. The second question, to which the first leads, pertains to the relationship of this 'truth' to the world of reality: Are the valid truths a realm of their own, or are they merely an expression of what we might call 'the essences of the real'? This second question discloses the problem of reality. But it also immediately raises the third question: How do such universally valid truths or universal essences relate to that aspect of the real that seems most real to us—namely, the concrete, individual diversity and multiplicity of the real? Thus, the third question discloses the problem of individuality.

In all three questions, the philosophies prevailing before Kant sharply diverged. In the first problem, the problem of validity, an a priori rationalism and a purely a posteriori empiricism confronted each other. On the one side was a philosophy in which 'truth' signified something suspended in itself, shining in the solitary depths of the mind without any connection to the experience of reality. On the other side was a philosophy in which 'truth' meant nothing more than a conceptual expression for inherently changing sensory impressions, and which, for that reason, was as mutable as these impressions.

Both tendencies essentially continued in the following two problems. For if, according to the first tendency (a priori rationalism), there exists something like a realm of inherently suspended truths or ideas, then logically, this realm of immutability and clarity is the 'actual reality,' and the concrete reality of our experience is only apparent reality. In other words, for the second question (the problem of reality), the answer appears as a system of so-called 'rational reality.' For the third question (the problem of individuality), the answer appears as the closed system of a 'universal reality'—i.e., the consistent exclusion of the reality of naïve experience. If, however, according to the second tendency (a posteriori empiricism), there exists only something like a constantly changing sensory experience of a constantly changing reality, then any attempt at approaching a so-called knowledge of 'essential reality' is an illusion or at least a fiction that perhaps has some pragmatic value—i.e., is useful or even necessary for certain practical achievements. In other words, for the second question (the problem of reality), the answer presents itself as an unsystematic 'experience' of unfathomable reality. For the third question (the problem of individuality), it presents itself as a consistent relativism and historicism, an unsystematic juxtaposition and succession of discretely limited individual experiences. In a nutshell, Wolff and Hume are radically opposed to each other.

Kant's solution, on the other hand, can be expressed in the phrase: unity in the 'transcendental subject' or, more precisely, unity as 'transcendental subject.' The term 'subject' puts the accent on the world of experience: a mass of experience[1] (i.e., the

---

1. *Erfahrungsgröße.*—Trans.

human being) is the unity of the world as divided between ideal and real, universal and individual. 'Transcendental' subject, however (in contrast to 'empirical subject'), elevates this mass of experience beyond the contingent realm of experience and, in this respect, emphasizes the a priori domain of validity that is characteristic of rationalism: the subject of the world's unity is not the individual, concrete human being but is instead the 'human in itself,' the heretofore purely cultural mass of 'humanity' now regarded as a philosophical mass.

*

The problem of validity.

The question of the problem of validity is: How can we explain that, on the one hand, our judgments necessarily aim at something absolutely valid—at 'absolute truth'—while on the other hand, this 'absolute truth' seems to be nothing more than the current expression of the interpenetration of contingent impressions and influences from the external world, blended with the personal attitudes and moods of the concrete, individual I who perceives and judges? This is initially the sense of Kant's question: "How are synthetic a priori judgments possible?" 'Synthetic' judgments, i.e., experiential judgments, but 'a priori,' i.e., experiential judgments that claim categorical[2] (i.e., absolute) validity. For Kant, both are self-evident presuppositions: first, that there is absolute truth, but second, that this truth shines forth in and through concrete experience. Kant's question is about the 'how'—i.e., the interior principle for this antithetical interplay[3]— and the interior principle for this interplay is what he calls the 'transcendental subject.' The mystery of the human being is that he himself is the unity between the 'intelligible world' (i.e., the world of absolute truth) and the 'sensory world' (i.e., the world

2. *schlechthinige.*—Trans.
3. *gegensätzlichen Ineinander.*—Trans.

of mutable experience). Therefore, he is the 'lawgiver of nature,' indeed, something like the 'demiurge'—i.e., the constant creator of unity from the antitheses in an 'infinite progress,' humanity in the human being.

This new unity, however, has an ambiguous significance, and the fate of this ambiguity becomes the tragic fate of the solution itself.

The 'human' as unity can once again be understood from the side of concrete humanity, and this interpretation no doubt corresponds to one aspect of Kant's solution—namely, the aspect that emphasizes the living concreteness of thinking against the abstract 'in itself' of contemporary rationalism: a subjective a priori against an abstract, objective a priori. But precisely this subjective a priori leads almost inevitably, step by step, to conceiving the objective relationships between the objective contents of thought as purely an 'expression' of its subjective laws. As a first stage (perhaps already in Kant himself, at least in some places), a sort of *functional logicism* arises, i.e., a conception according to which the objectivity in the contents of thought is only the objectivity of formal laws of thought—in the end not objectivity but the absolutization of the objective in formal law[4]. But, as a result of the inner logic of this conception, this stage (represented, for example, by *Salomon Maimon*) does not last.

Once the accent is placed on formal, subjective thinking, an initial logicism necessarily soon turns into a genuine *psychologism*. The so-called objective laws of thought ultimately appear as laws of the natural, organic constitution of the human being, and two possibilities for the development of thought open up almost automatically: first (and this is still a last remnant of objectivity), the psychologism that produces a typology of thinking (such as in *Dilthey* and *Simmel*[5]); but then the genuine psychologism that

4. *Objecktivation.*—Trans.
5. Wilhelm Dilthey and Georg Simmel.—Trans.

dissolves the logical laws of thought into laws of the psychophysical organism, and finally, dissolves thinking altogether into a higher, sensory common feeling (in the 'sensualism'[6] of the middle and end of the last century), which ultimately appears simply (in Freud's theory of cognition) as a 'sublimation' of purely *biological* states.

Thus, in a straightforward development of one of Kant's truly fundamental ideas, a stage is reached that signifies the most stark contradiction to his own fundamental tendency, in which, for him, the 'intelligible world' shines as the true world over against the 'sensory world.' This is the world that, guided by the categories of 'pure reason' and the postulates of 'practical reason,' at least asymptotically radiates as the 'true world' before the mind of the founder of German idealism. That is, the innermost tendency of this system is to advance from the world of the senses into the pure world of the mind.

Let us, therefore, try to do justice to this side of Kant's thought. 'The human' considered as a 'unity' must, as indeed we saw in the introductory remarks, not be understood as the individual, empirical human being but as 'the human in a human being'[7], as the 'pure human,' the 'human in itself,' 'humanity' in an epistemological sense—that is, as the 'transcendental subject.' It is the aspect of Kant's solution that confronts the sensualist empiricism of his time, emphasizing the 'objective in itself' of thought's contents, knowing truth only as 'absolute truth.' In this respect, the vigorous reaction of the neo-Kantianism of the Marburg school against all psychologism—i.e., against the dissolution of thought's contents into symbols of vital processes (as it emerged precisely as a consequence of the 'subjective a priori')— is truly grounded in Kant himself. From here, the Marburg 'pure method' is, therefore, not a first step toward the dissolution of

6. *Sensismus.*—Trans.
7. *der "Mensch des Menschen."*—Trans.

19

the 'content,' but rather the beginning of the corrective against such dissolution—i.e., the beginning of that 'objectivism' that has reached its peak in the strict objectivism of *phenomenology.*

Initially, this objectivism is opposed to a relativistic psychologism, the objectivity of the 'method' of thinking, the 'universally valid' and 'intrinsically valid' 'pure method,' which then—in the completion of the struggle against psychologism through Husserl's *Logical Investigations*—culminated in the objectivity of thought's contents themselves, in the absolute objectivity of 'pure essences,' which thought encounters only in 'intuition.' However, this tendency of the 'logical-objective' expands both in [1] recent cognitive psychology, which, contrary to older sensualism, explicitly aims for the goal of sense-free 'pure thinking,' and in [2] the Adlerian individual psychology sharply opposed to Freudian biologism. The latter, in contrast to Freud, interprets the sensate and biological almost solely as symbols of the spiritual orientation of man's knowledge and striving (a person's 'meaningful goals').

Therefore, from this second tendency of Kant's solution, the more recent objectivism—even if it may perceive itself (especially in phenomenology) as 'an opponent of Kant'—is, in truth, only a logical development of his thought. But viewed precisely as Kant's logical development, this tendency tears apart the original dichotomy at the heart of Kant's unity from the opposite side as before. For this development of Kant's objectivism ultimately culminates in a doctrine where thinking is the contemplative vision of 'given essences' in the absolute sense. However, this is in stark contradiction to Kant's teaching on the activity and spontaneity of thought. So, we now see from the other side the contradiction that was revealed to us before on the side of the 'subjective a priori.' The objectivism of Kant's thought, carried through to its logical issue, contradicts the subjective activism of its spontaneity when it, too, is carried through to its conclusion.

In other words, the present sharp antitheses between active subjectivism and passive objectivism in the problem of validity are nothing but the inner contradiction in Kant's own solution torn wide open.

*

The problem of reality.

The question of the problem of reality is: How can we explain that, on the one hand, the so-called 'reality' we speak of and reckon with is, in crucial respects, a construct[8] that emerges only through our thought processes and is thus something like a 'rational reality'—and that, on the other hand, precisely because of this, 'reality in itself' increasingly eludes cognition, eventually becoming something like the 'counter-rational,' the 'ignotum X,' the 'unknown world,' even the 'irrational X' of a 'chaotic-demonic world'? This question leads us to the deeper meaning of Kant's question—"How are synthetic a priori judgments possible?"—in the sense that addresses the problem of the knowledge of reality itself. How is it possible that we can know reality 'rationally,' i.e., discern the essential structures of reality through the atomistic and chaotic realm of pure sensory impressions, and yet still thereby know 'reality,' i.e., not our knowledge, but the world and life that stand as objects counterposed to our knowledge?

For Kant, both are again self-evident presuppositions: first, that our knowledge aims at 'reality in itself,' and second, equally, that such knowledge shapes reality 'rationally.' His question is about the 'how'—i.e., the inner principle for this antithetical interplay—and he again, in a deeper sense, names as the inner principle for this interplay the 'transcendental subject.'

It is the deeper mystery of the human being that he, in his 'idea,' in 'humanity in itself,' is the real center of reality. The world is directed toward human understanding, and therefore, its

8. *Gebilde.*—Trans.

21

being shaped in and through 'thinking in itself'—that is, through the 'pure categories' of human thinking—means this 'creation of reality' ultimately does not signify an antithesis to 'reality in itself' but its fulfillment. It is thus understandable that, for Kant, an existential subsistence[9] of 'things in themselves,' i.e., of reality outside human thinking, is self-evident—but equally, this 'reality prior to thought' has no significance for him and can be coldly dismissed as the 'ignotum X.' It must be precisely such an 'ignotum X' because 'in itself' it is only chaos that first receives its inner form in and through the human being: it first becomes the world in and through the human being as its 'demiurge,' in 'infinite progress,' the world through 'humanity in the human being.'

As in the problem of validity, this new unity once again has an ambiguous significance, and the fate of this ambiguity becomes the tragic fate of the solution itself.

The solution represented by the phrase 'world in and through the human being' can emphasize 'in and through the human being,' and this interpretation undoubtedly corresponds to one aspect of Kant's solution, indeed precisely the one that, for the popular understanding of Kant, almost appears as *the* Kantian doctrine. It is the theory of reality of *German idealism*, for which the so-called 'rational' or 'ideal' reality is the only one. For German idealism in the progression from Fichte to Hegel, the real world increasingly becomes the dialectic of the pure idea, which not only shines forth in the I but ultimately is the I: the pure idea as absolute spirit—i.e., as the transcendental subject. For German idealism in the form of Marburg and Baden *neo-Kantianism*, even this reality of the world is extinguished in favor of the sole reality of pure method or pure values. 'Rational reality' has merged into 'pure rationality,' 'ideal reality' into the 'pure ideality' of the method or valuation.

However, this marks a stage in the straightforward

9. *existentielles Bestehen.*—Trans.

development of a genuinely fundamental idea of Kant's that stands in irreconcilable contradiction to that other fundamental tendency, in which Kant (in opposition to all 'top down' rationalism that sought to give empirical experience its due) asserts the existence of a trans-subjective reality as a self-evident presupposition. In this fundamental tendency, the doctrine of the categories almost signifies a kind of degradation of human thinking—a reduction to recognizing an aspect of the world, namely, the world 'for me,' and the failure of a proud knowledge of the 'world in itself.' In other words: the development of the Kant of the 'ideal world' contradicts the Kant of the "I had to deny knowledge . . ."

So, let's try to do justice to this other side of Kant's thought. The 'world in and through the human being' must indeed, when stress is put on the 'world,' at least 'also' be understood as the projection of a 'world in itself' beyond all rational or categorical comprehension and delimitation. A development arises, then, that could well bear the common name of *irrationalism* and for which Kant himself, to a certain extent, paves the way. For Kant, a kind of breakthrough of the strict limits of 'pure reason' can take place, or at least is initiated, only through 'practical reason,' i.e., through the experience of the will: "I had to deny knowledge for the sake of faith." In other words, it is the [line of] development from *Schopenhauer's* irrational intuition (for whom, for this very reason, the 'will' is the real 'thing in itself') through *Nietzsche* up to *Bergson's* vital intuition.

And yet, in a development running parallel to this, the powerfully growing *positive sciences* rise up against the German idealism of the 'purely rational ideality' and (proceeding right up to the philosophical corollary of *materialism*) take for 'true reality' something that bears a minimum of 'rationality.' But this development, too, is born of Kant, from the Kant of "I had to deny knowledge . . ."

And finally (raising the paradox of this development to its

utmost), even that phenomenological 'overcoming of the systematic Kant'—as most impressively embodied in the legacy
of the last disciple of Marburg neo-Kantianism, Nicolai Hartmann—reveals itself to be a real development of Kant (starting
from the Kant who restricts knowledge). For what else is the
'trans-intelligible' of 'infinitely existing' reality that transcends all
seemingly creative knowing and thinking other than a making
explicit—i.e., an explicit emphasis on Kant's notion of the incomprehensibility of the 'world in itself'?

As a result of this threefold development, the image of the
absolutely 'irrational reality' now emerges as the true reality. The
principle would thus be: reality is experienced as reality not to the
extent that reality is in 'rational ideality,' but to the extent that it
shatters the confines and simplifications of such 'rational ideality'
and extends beyond it into an ungraspable distance. However,
this (which, as we have seen, is itself a straightforward development of Kant) is in open contradiction to the equally undeniably Kantian idea of the 'intelligible world' as the true world: the
world of chaotic reality is only the 'matter' of the formed reality of
the 'actually existing' (Plato's *ontōs on*) 'intelligible world.'

So, even here, the present sharp antitheses between optimistic humanism[10] ('the world through the human being') and tragic
cosmism ('the world beyond the human being') in the problem
of reality are nothing but the inner contradiction in Kant's own
solution torn wide open.

*

The problem of individuality.

The question of the problem of individuality is: How can we
explain that—on the one hand (in the completion of the idea
of 'rational reality')—reality, in its more precise structure, appears as a fabric of universal laws, structures, essences, or types,

10. *Humanitarismus.*—Trans.

against which the concrete, unique, individual, and historical is reduced to an 'exemplar' or at least an 'intersected phenomenon'[11] of these universal laws, etc.? But—on the other hand (in the completion of the idea of 'irrational reality')—precisely thereby, 'the being of reality in itself'[12] in its aspect of bewildering diversity, peculiar singularity, and unpredictability of the individual and historical increasingly eludes knowledge, and the arbitrary-lawless, the unpredictable-revolutionary, becomes absolute? This question leads us to the last, deepest sense of Kant's question, "How are synthetic a priori judgments possible?" For 'synthetic a priori judgments' aim ultimately, by their very nature, at a 'lawful' knowledge of reality. This means a dual comprehension of reality: one within its unalterable and hence 'a priori' valid and 'a priori' intelligible system of laws, where the individual appears merely as 'quantitative,' i.e., a simple 'application' of universal laws; and the other in the 'concrete-empirical' reality, where, conversely, a multitude of incomparable and unrepeatable qualitative-individual aspects constitutes what is 'essential' and 'primary.' Against this backdrop, the whole system of universal laws presents itself precisely as a 'secondary abstraction.'

For Kant, both are again self-evident presuppositions: first, that our closer knowledge and exploration of reality aims at the 'ultimate structure of laws,' which is the 'deepest essence' of all coexistence and succession of the concrete-historical-individual[13]; second, that the tendency of our knowledge of the fabric of reality has its meaning in 'reality itself,' not laws for the sake of laws, but laws as a means to understand the individual-concrete-historical[14]—and thereby has an object of knowledge that seems fundamentally to escape confinement within laws. Kant's question is about the 'how'—that is, the

11. *Kreuzungsphänomen.*—Trans.
12. *Realitäts-Sosein an sich.*—Trans.
13. *Konkret-Geschichtlich-Individuellen.*—Trans.
14. *Individuell-Konkret-Geschichtlichen.*—Trans.

inner principle for this antithetical interplay—and the 'transcendental subject' now appears in its deepest sense as this innermost principle.

Because in the problem of reality as a whole, 'the human being' was posited as the unified basis of the knowledge of 'rational reality' and 'reality in itself,' this role of a unified foundation now reaches its completion in the problem of individuality—i.e., in the problem of the more detailed structure of reality. For the fundamental nature of Kant's 'human in the human being' is precisely that it is within itself the mysterious unity of 'human in itself' and the 'concrete human being': thus, within itself, it is the unity of 'universal' and 'individual' that is sought for the solution to the problem of individuality (according to what has just been said). In other words, the innermost essence of the 'transcendental subject' is precisely that it is the solution to the problem of the 'universal' and the 'individual'—i.e., the problem of individuality.

Only in the solution to the problem of individuality does the full meaning of Kant's solution unfold. Because fundamentally every solution (to the problems of validity and reality) lies in 'the human being,' 'humanity in the human being' (in 'infinite progress') is the unity in which the tension between 'universal' and 'individual' in the entire world is bound and resolved: the tension of the coexistence and succession of 'universal' and 'individual' in the coexistence of the world's resting fundamental structure—as well as in the succession of its historical course—is ultimately bound and resolved in and through the unity of the 'universal human' and the 'concrete human being' of humanity. The 'infinite progress' (wherein the world actualizes the 'universal' in the 'individual') finds its unity in the 'infinite progress' in which, in the [individual] human being, 'humanity' becomes 'human': the world (in its highest sense) in and through the human being as its 'demiurge,' in 'infinite progress,' the world through 'humanity in the human being.'

But just as in the problem of validity and reality, this new unity has an ambiguous significance, and the fate of this ambiguity becomes the tragic fate of the solution and reaches the apex of the tragedy of Kant's solution as a whole (because the ambiguity resides here in the inner sense of 'humanity in the human being' itself, in the innermost tension of the 'transcendental subject' between the 'I in itself' and the 'concrete I').

'Humanity in the human being' can be understood as a solution to the problem of individuality in reality with the emphasis placed on 'humanity . . . ' It is then the logical conclusion of 'rational, ideal reality' in the problem of reality as a whole. It is also the logical outcome of Kant's transcendentalism as a whole. Because as much as it also pertains to the 'world in and through the human being,' in this formula, the 'world' is truly understood as the world of 'ultimate connections,' and 'the human being' is understood as the 'universal-human in the human being.' Kant consciously aims to restrain the rising, boundless individualism (originating from the Renaissance and partly the Reformation) that threatens to inundate all rigorous science and strict ethics by imposing the constraints of strict laws. The categories in which the seemingly creative subject accomplishes this 'creative shaping' are 'a priori'—i.e., independent of the concrete, individual human being. And the 'autonomy' of the will is also not an autonomy of the concrete individual will (for in the sphere of appearance, there is no freedom) but of the will of the 'human in itself.' Indeed, by the fact that this 'human in itself' bears the strict character of an 'ideal,' toward which the concrete, individual human being only ever 'strives' in 'infinite progress' (without reaching it), through this consciously sundered chasm between the 'human in itself' and the 'concrete, individual human being' (to which Kant's doctrine of 'radical evil' as the philosophical expression of the Lutheran doctrine of original sin is added)—through this, at least in Kant, the 'foundation' has been laid for that severe disenfranchisement[15] of the concrete individual, wherein it appears almost as the 'impure' in comparison with the 'pure' of the universal. In other words, we see the development of the problem of individuality as it unfolds not only in Fichte but also in the trajectory from Schelling to Schopenhauer to Hartmann, finding its connecting center in Hegel.

In *Fichte*: there is an apparent positive valuation of the concrete individual[16], inasmuch as Fichte specifically emphasizes the I and focuses on a philosophy of history; but a positive valuation whose outcome is a complete objectification of the 'absolute I' into an 'objective order.'

In *Schelling* (primarily the earlier Schelling) and then expressly in *Schopenhauer* and *Hartmann*: indeed, there is a distinction of the I against a world of ideas or the unconscious, but it is the distinction of the sinful and fallen against a primal innocence (Schelling), or the restless-wandering against life-liberated tranquility (Schopenhauer), or sickness against health (Hartmann).

In *Hegel*: certainly, there is an attempt to save both the dynamism and vitality of the individual and the immutability of the universal, but such that the individual becomes the actual 'dialectic' of the universal, not only in its factual movement but also in its rational—i.e., logically necessary movement.

And as an extension and outflow of these basic philosophical orientations: in the realm of science, there is the undisputed primacy of 'universal' sciences (from biology to psychology and cultural sciences), for which the individual is only an 'application' or 'intersected phenomenon' of universal laws; and in practical life, there is the undisputed primacy of state and society before which the individual has only the value of an 'obedient subject' (whether facing an all-powerful monarchy or an all-powerful democracy) or that of a 'flawless member of society.'

15. *ärgere Entrechtung.*—Trans.
16. *Individuell-Konkreten.*—Trans.

But with this, in a straightforward development of the primal sense of Kant's transcendentalism overall, a stage is reached
in which an equally 'primal sense' of the same transcendentalism
is vehemently denied: Kant against Kant. We mean that primal
sense derived from Rousseau's 'natural man' (in contrast to the
man of the state, society, and universal science): the 'pure man' in
the sense of the human unfolding naturally from his innate I, the
ideal of humanity and of the world in 'pure nature,' which represents an original feeling and experience of Kant against the rationalistic ideal of 'calculating culture.' It is the *homo in silvis*, the
'pure, free man,' the archetype of the 'human rights' of the French
Revolution, meaning the man who has his philosophical form in
Kant's 'subjective a priori.' Here, we can see the contradiction in
its most acute form: for precisely that 'rational ideal reality,' whose
logical outcome[17] is the 'reality of universality' just described, has
this very 'subjective a priori' as its correlative foundation in the
problem of validity. In short, since our initial interpretation of a
'reality of universality' ultimately traces back to this 'subjective a
priori,' but on the other hand, as we just observed, this 'subjective
a priori' opposes a 'reality of universality,' our initial interpretation of Kant's solution to the problem of individuality carries its
negation within itself from the outset.

Let us attempt the other possible interpretation of Kant's
solution, as it at least implicitly contains the 'subjective a priori'
against the backdrop of Rousseau's understanding of humanity.
Our general formulation of Kant's solution to the problem of
individuality, 'humanity in the human being,' can also be understood with the emphasis on '. . . in the human being.' By consciously speaking of a 'Copernican revolution,' Kant undoubtedly
represents the same ethos and pathos in which *Rousseau's* 'natural
man' rebels against the coercive network of 'general ties.' Kant's
protest as a philosopher of religion against 'statutory' religion is,

17. *Zu-ende-Denkung.*—Trans.

from this perspective, only the final expression of his fundamental protest against a dependence of humans on collective structures[18]. In Kant's fundamental epistemological formula—which inverts the old relationship of the 'subject as the receiver of the object' (who is therefore dependent on, ordered to, and subordinated to the object) to the new relationship of 'the object as the creation of the subject' (and therefore in the free power of the subject)—in this fundamental formula, the old Reformation 'protest' lives on as the 'protest' of subjective 'inwardness' against objective 'churchliness'[19].

With this, Kant appears, quite naturally, as the true father of those movements that have rebelled in past centuries and are currently rebelling in our century against a supremacy of 'collective structures.' He is the father of those movements, ranging from their mildest form in Baden's value-Kantianism[20] to their sharpest form in the individualism of [Ernst] Troeltsch and Simmel. He is likewise the father of their practical manifestations, from class-based individualistic socialism to the personal individualism of Nietzsche and [Max] Stirner.

For the first, more scientific movements, no special explanation is needed. The literature of the *Baden school* consciously builds on the Kant of 'practical reason'—i.e., on that Kant who, in contrast to the stronger aspect of the universal law in the categories of the Kant of 'pure reason,' emphasizes the freely-willed vitality of the subject. *Troeltsch* and *Simmel*, while engaging in something like a struggle against 'Kantianism,' fundamentally do so in the name of Kant against neo-Kantianism, as Simmel clearly states and Troeltsch hints at, especially in his late works.

Class-based, individualistic *socialism* indeed has a strong element of universality within itself and entails the adoption of the Hegelian 'whole,' which is merely an 'idea-whole' rebaptized as an

18. *Allgemeingebilden.*—Trans.
19. *Kirchlichkeit.*—Trans.
20. *Wertkantianismus.*—Trans.

'economic-whole.' In it, however, the protest of the 'natural man' and the 'creative man' against the 'man of culture and possession' is more strongly alive. That is, the protest of the person who only recognizes the value of 'one's own labor'—and sees everything else solely as a consequence and function of this, thus viewing all objective aspects as functions of the subjective—against the person who is a passive 'bearer' of the objective, a 'bearer' of possessions and values that he 'bequeaths' to other passive bearers. In other words, behind the socialist protest of the 'person of labor' against the 'person of possession,' the Kantian protest becomes visible, the protest of the individual against collective structures: Kant is thus, in a true sense, the father of socialism.

The personal individualism of *Nietzsche* and *Stirner*, viewed from this perspective, unmistakably bears its Kantian origin on its forehead. In its deepest depths, it is somewhat like Rousseau's man taken up by Kant in its 'pure form.' But with this, again in a straightforward development of an undeniably primal sense of Kantian transcendentalism as a whole, the earlier primal sense of the same transcendentalism (which emphasized the objective-universal) is most sharply denied. The chasm that we had to consider in the examination of the first sense of Kant's solution now gapes at us from the other side.

Therefore, even in this ultimate problem, today's sharp antitheses between communal universalism (the individual as a passive derivation of the universal) and anti-communal individualism (everything universal at the mercy of the individual's will) in the problem of individuality are nothing other than the inner contradiction in Kant's own solution torn wide open.

II

THOMAS CONSIDERED IN LIGHT OF THIS ANTITHESIS

How should we interpret this situation? Is there a Kantian revolution in this Kant crisis, as formulated by Nicolai Hartmann on the occasion of Kant's jubilee: from a 'systematic Kant' of solutions to an 'aporetic Kant' of ultimate questions? Or does the Kantian revolution go even further, as seems to be the case in Eugen Herrigel's works on Kant: perhaps right on through an aporetic Kant and into the problems of ancient philosophy?

We evidently need to answer the question through an immanent analysis of our first part.

*

The problem of validity.

Kant saw the solution in the human being. The human as a living, concrete, individual human being is the foundation of the dynamic vitality inherent in all knowledge of truth. The creatively vital aspect in humans is the basis for the creative process of recognizing truth: thinking as an act rooted in the concrete individual human as the agent. 'Humanity' in this concrete human being—the 'transcendental subject' in the 'empirical subject'—is the foundation of the objectivity and immutability that inheres in the same knowledge of truth. The immutable-universal in human beings is the basis of the immutable-universal in the recognition of truth: thinking as receptive is anchored in the human as the pure 'appearance only' of the universally immutable 'human in itself.'

The analysis of the crisis that has occurred in this solution yielded, as a result, a clear view of the sundered contradiction of this solution. The history of Kant's solution revealed itself to be the history of the unfolding of its hidden antitheses up to the point of open contradiction. Its unfolded active subjectivism (of the 'a priori' as 'subjective a priori') turned into a stark rejection of the objective element Kant intended to accompany it. Conversely, its unfolded passive subjectivism (of the 'a priori' as 'objective a priori') became a stark rejection of the subjective element Kant also intended to accompany it.

It is true: from the conflict of schools, which has ended or is still ending in mutual dissolution, the image of Kant's original problem emerges clearer than ever. It is indeed a reawakening of the 'aporetic' Kant in the demise of the 'systematic' Kant. But is the meaning of the current situation exhausted by this? Wasn't Kant's positive and explicit endeavor aimed at dispelling and binding the problem within the unity of the human being, so much so that for his philosophy, the absolute emphasis is on the human being, on the 'human within the human being'—i.e., on 'humanity in the human being,' on 'humanity'? Both the absolute character of truth and its relative character, its divine character and creaturely character, is one in the human being qua human— the human who (as the *Lectures on Metaphysics* repeatedly states) is both creator and creature. Consequently, this human is not only the sole center of creation but also the sole center of both creator and creation, understood as the (from this perspective) 'limit concept' of the one 'humanity.' But wasn't this the essence of Kant's solution, fundamentally addressing the problem of validity and unfolding and culminating in the problems of reality and individuality?

If, however, this is the case (and it is the case, as the first part of our study tells us), can we still speak of an 'awakening of the aporetic Kant' as the true positive meaning of today's 'Kantian revolution'? Kant stands or falls with the 'transcendental subject' as the ultimate unity of antitheses. Only from this collapse does that problem reemerge, for which the 'transcendental subject' was supposed to be the solution.

However, this is the problem of Thomas Aquinas. In a significant difference from Kant, he does not close the problem of validity within the human being but keeps it wide open: the problem between creative thinking and receptive thinking, the problem, as he calls it, between a certain absoluteness of 'truth' shining in creative, active thinking, 'veritas in intellectu,' and the relativity of this truth to events independent of thought, 'veritas' as 'adaequatio intellectus ad rem.' This is the problem between thinking as a creative shaping of 'truth' from sensory data ('intellectus agens') and thinking as a pure, contemplative reception of 'truth in itself' ('intellectus possibilis'). The major difference between Thomas Aquinas and Kant is that Thomas neither wants to nor can eliminate this ultimate problem and therefore does not succumb to the temptation to surpass it through an artificial unity within humans (only to have it escalate into an explosive conflict). For Thomas Aquinas, the problem of validity is the fundamental aspect of simple creatureliness, and in this fundamental aspect, the gaze turns to God beyond humanity. Human thinking, it is true, has a 'creative-receptive' character. But the 'creative' in this interplay is not the 'Absolute,' is not God, as Kant's solution ultimately suggests. Rather, the interplay of 'creative-receptive' in thinking is the first glimmer of the 'analogia entis,' which constitutes the fundamental relationship between God and creature: 'God-likeness (in the creative) in God-unlikeness (in the receiving).'

*

The problem of reality.

Kant, in turn, saw the solution in the human being. The human is at the center of the world. Therefore, 'reality' in its proper sense, in the sense of 'rational, ideal reality,' is something that arises only in and through humans, as human thinking creatively shapes the incoming impressions of the world into this 'rational, ideal reality.' Thus, indeed, 'reality' is only recognizable in its 'for humans,' not in its pure 'in itself.' But this 'in itself' precisely has the inner meaning of pure 'matter' for the shaping of the 'actual world' in and through human beings.

The analysis of the crisis that ensued from this solution resulted in a clear view of the gaping contradiction in it. The history of Kant's solution showed itself to be the history of the unfolding of this contradiction. Its unfolded active humanism (the world shaped by and through humans) turned into a stern rejection of Kant's concurrently intended element of the world's almost diabolical unknowability and unpredictability. Conversely, the resulting tragic cosmism (the world as chaos beyond the shaping human) became a stark denial of Kant's equally intended element of the ideal formation of the world.

It is once again true: the image of Kant's original problem emerges more clearly than ever from the conflict of schools, a conflict that has either ended or is still in the process of ending through mutual dissolution. The contrast becomes evident between that primal rationalistic element, where 'pure reason,' or humanistic reason, appears as the light that 'enlightens' the world darkened by a 'dark supernaturalism' into noonday brightness. This is contrasted with the indelibly primal, Lutheran element, persisting despite all rationalism, in which the same world reveals itself as the world that is primally sinful and diabolical. This world can be so little 'enlightened' by 'pure reason' that so-called 'pure reason' is nothing but the sharpest expression of its primal sin and primal demonism[21], identified as 'whore reason.' Humanistic reason, or human consciousness, becomes merely the keenest awareness of this world's primal damnation. It is truly a reawakening of the 'aporetic' Kant in the death of the 'systematic' Kant.

But is the meaning of the present situation exhausted by this? Wasn't Kant's positive and explicit endeavor in our problem aimed at resolving not only the philosophical conflict between rationalism and empiricism but even more profoundly (at least in its ultimate depths) the deeper conflict outlined above? This deeper conflict is between the humanist-rational world and the demonic-irrational world, between a world shaped by humans and a world against humans. Kant sought to resolve this conflict in and through the same 'transcendental subject' that constitutes

21. *Ur-Dämonie.*—Trans.

the basis for solving the problem of validity. Humanity, seen as the 'ideal human in itself,' becomes the formal principle[22] of the humanist-rational world. Conversely, the empirical-concrete human—viewed as the 'empirical subject' and thus as the eternally flawed manifestation of the 'ideal human in itself'—acts as an unimprovable and ineradicably original sinner against the 'ideal human.' This concrete human, identified as 'sinner,' becomes the foundational principle of the demonic-unreal world, the world of sin. So, according to Kant's at least unconscious intentions, doesn't the *absolute* accent come to rest on this human, the absolute accent of the ultimate, all-conditioning unity of plurality and antitheses[23], at least insofar as the absolute accent (as a certain last irremediable tragedy of this 'humanity in the human being') unmistakably bears the countenance of a mythological tragedy[24]—i.e., a god-like tragedy, the tragedy that is fitting only to a final, all-conditioning ground of unity for the fragmented world?

If, however, this is the case (and it is the case, as the first part of our study tells us), can we still speak of an 'awakening of the aporetic Kant' as the true positive meaning of today's 'Kantian revolution'? Kant stands and falls with the 'transcendental subject'— the ultimate unity of antitheses, whose highest creative capacity is enacted in the unity of these tragic antitheses, a unity experienced in all its profound and hidden tragedy as a mythic-tragic agon[25] (and in this sense Nietzsche's 'will to power' is of Kant's lineage). Only from the collapse of this Kantian-Nietzschean *Übermensch* does that problem rise again for which the 'transcendental subject' was supposed to be the solution.

The problem of reality, as it presented itself to Kant, was twofold, or better: it had both a foreground and a background. The foreground of the problem lay in the antithesis between the

22. *Formgrund.*—Trans.
23. *Gegensätzlichkeit.*—Trans.
24. *Macht-Tragik.*—Trans.
25. *Tragik macht-tragischen.*—Trans.

rationalism of a priori constructed reality and the empiricism of reality ultimately incomprehensible or at least only asymptotically attainable from the chaos of experience. The background of the problem, on the other hand, existed in the antithesis between the humanist rationalism of the enlightened world of reason and the reason-condemning Lutheranism of the demonic world of sin. And as we saw: only through the background problem does the foreground problem become that sharp, irreconcilable antithesis between optimistic humanism and tragic cosmism (as the problem of reality showed us in the first part at the end).

With this, however, it becomes apparent how the 'absolutization' that constitutes the explosive substance of the solution is already inherent in the problem itself. For the humanist rationalism of the enlightened world of reason, which stands behind philosophical rationalism, needs no closer analysis: the 'enlightened reason' is the usurpation of the Johannine 'God is light' for humanity. But the same applies to the reason-condemning Lutheranism of the demonic world of sin. For what lies behind such a fearful judgment of condemnation over God's creation if not an immense consciousness of judgment (conscious to the Reformers!) upon the humans who pronounce such a judgment [over the world]? The rationalism and empiricism of the purely philosophical problem are so extreme because the extremity of a 'human as God' permeates them. 'Extreme' indeed! If humans, in one way or another, either through the direct 'desire to be God' with a direct consciousness of power or through the indirect 'desire to merge into God' with an indirect need for power—seeking to seize the power of the 'other' by merging into it—claim the omnipotence and fullness of God for themselves, the result is not an 'Absolute' but rather its caricature: the 'Extreme'[26].

It should therefore be clear how, in Thomas Aquinas as the

---

26. *das 'Extrem.'*—Trans.

thinker of ecstatic creatureliness[27], this problem is cleansed, purified into the simple antithesis between a true orientation of the world toward the human spirit and an equally true orientation of the human spirit as a 'member of the world' toward the world as the overarching 'All' encompassing it. It is true: Aquinas's genuinely Aristotelian doctrine of abstraction states that the 'essential nature' of the real world is purified through creative thinking (*intellectus agens!*) into the purity of a 'world of essences.' For Thomas, the system of (ontological) 'essential forms' is the essential nature of the world, and simultaneously, it is the creative aspect of the 'intellectus agens,' through which this essential nature is distilled into purity. But for the same Thomas, the seemingly creative thinking of the human spirit always remains bound to the senses (*nihil est in intellectu, quod non fuerit in sensu*[28]), and all creaturely thinking in general (even that of a creaturely 'pure spirit') always remains 'in potentia'—i.e., always bound to the growing apprehension of a world that essentially transcends and floods this apprehension, never exhausting the world. Only God, who does not 'become' but 'is,' comprehends the world because He knows it 'from the ground up,' from the primal ground from which it sprang, from Himself: knowing Himself through and through, the Unfathomable comprehends (in comprehending Himself alone) the riddle of the world, which He alone resolves because it came from Him.

So, what is ultimate in man's relation to the world is that he recognizes and humbly acknowledges his obligation toward it, meaning his task to continually work on it, but equally his submission to it—i.e., to the gift of its ever richer abundance, which discloses itself to the person who opens himself to it simply and without restraint. In other words, the 'creative-receptive' nature of the problem of validity intensifies itself, and thereby,

---

27. *unverkrampften Geschöpflichkeit.*—Trans.
28. nothing is in the intellect that was not [first] in the senses. See *De Veritate* 2.3.—Trans.

the illumination of the 'analogy of being' comprehending this antithesis shines more brightly too. For it shines in the antithesis between [1] the God-likeness of a 'person as All' that creates and so comprehends the world, and [2] the God-unlikeness of a 'person as Member' who receives from the world and, in the process, ultimately comes to comprehend the world's incomprehensibility: God-likeness in God-unlikeness.

*

The problem of individuality.

As we saw, the culmination and synthesis of Kant's solution is found here. As the final outcome to the solution of the problem of reality 'in the human being,' the juxtaposition of reality's universal and individual aspects (as the more detailed 'essence' of reality) finds its unity and resolution in the unity of the transcendental and empirical subjects in the human being, in the 'human in the human being,' which, taken quite literally, results in a 'doubling of the I.'

However, the resulting analysis of the crisis ensuing from this solution had to escalate to the utmost, as we just saw for the problems of validity and reality. Because the root of the collapse of Kant's solution in these two initial problems was always the sundered contradiction between the 'human in itself' and the 'concrete human,' a contradiction that was internally necessary because, with any mixing of the 'human in itself' with the 'concrete human,' the ideal-absoluteness of the former ceases to exist. For as we have also seen repeatedly, it is the 'ideality' of the 'human in itself,' not the ordinary ideality of an inner human ideal. Indeed, this ideality bears divine traits. It is absoluteness. It is God-as-humanity. But as we have also seen, it is God-as-humanity as a pole in an antithesis whose other extreme is [Lutheranism's] condemning rejection of the 'concrete human being.' This is because, in Kant's solution, the contradiction between the deification of humanity in humanist rationalism and the condemnation of humanity in original Lutheranism converges. So, if this contradictory unity of the 'human in the human being' as such—explicitly in the sense of its opposition between the 'human in itself' and the 'concrete human being'—is to lead to the solution of the problem of individuality in reality as a whole, then this solution can only bring forth the greatest and final chaos of the sundered contradiction. So, it is actually self-evident from the outset here that the history of Kant's solution is nothing but a history of its hidden antitheses evolving into open and contradictory conflicts. The unfolded communal universalism (where the individual is regarded as a passive offshoot of the universal) ultimately starkly contradicts the element Kant concurrently intended: the deeply rooted, almost revolutionary freedom of the individual. Conversely, the resulting anti-communal individualism (where everything universal is at the mercy of the individual's whims) starkly contradicts the element Kant equally intended: the singular 'human in itself' that alone 'ought to be'—i.e., the unity of 'humanity' as a universal.

Indeed, it is true here, or rather precisely here: from the dispute among schools, which has ended or is still ending in mutual dissolution, the image of Kant's original problem emerges clearer than ever. It is the image that we saw in the concluding discussion of the problem of reality: the problem between the 'human as God' of humanist rationalism and the 'human as enemy of God' of original Lutheranism. Here, however, the problem is even more acute since it has reached its terminus. Reality (viewed from this deepest problem) is the incurable rift between two 'Absolutes,' between the Absolute of community (in the humanity-God of rationalism) and the Absolute of the individual (in Lutheranism, where the One, condemning and bestowing grace, is the mono-causal[29] God whose innermost nature is that of the human

29. *alleinwirksamen.*—Trans.

40

who is only ever 'driven'). In this respect, it is a true reawakening of the 'aporetic' Kant in the demise of the 'systematic' Kant. It signifies the revival of the aporetic Kant in its sharpest perplexity—the perplexity that, stemming from the problem of Leibniz's *Monadology*, shapes the entire form of Kant. The problem at hand is the tension between the totality of the world as the 'Absolute Ground' (and hence 'a posteriori'—i.e., receptive, experiential thinking) and the depth of the I as the 'Absolute Ground' (and hence 'a priori'—i.e., thinking that creatively shapes [the world] according to inherent laws).

But is the meaning of the present situation exhausted by this? Wasn't the striving of Kant in our problem (as the conclusion of the first two problems) precisely and explicitly directed toward solving not only this problem but toward solving it through the unity of his 'transcendental subject'? Toward solving it (as we must consistently say in relation to what we just explained in the treatment of the problem of reality) in the philosophical foreground of the either-or between universalism and individualism, as well as in the religious background of the either-or between the divine ground of community and the divine ground of the I? But wasn't the decisive culmination of Kant's solution found precisely in solving this ultimate problem through the 'transcendental subject'? Isn't it here that the innermost concept of the 'transcendental' subject—its duplication into 'universal' ('human in itself') and 'individual' ('human in itself' as the meaning of the concrete human being)—was meant to represent the solution to the problem of individuality as a whole? In the problem of the aporetic Kant, the objective was to bridge the nearly Manichaean gap between community as the divine ground (embodied in the humanity-God of rationalism) and the I as the divine ground (found in Lutheranism's absolute immediacy of God to the I and within it). Simultaneously, the solution proposed by the systematic Kant explicitly aimed at uniting these contradictions through

41

the duplication of the 'transcendental subject.' Doesn't such a solution, first and foremost, establish the 'human in the human being' as the unity of these conflicting divine grounds, essentially becoming the focal point of the divine ground as a whole—more precisely, God as a whole (interpreted within the context of 'humanity' as God)? And second, doesn't the sundered contradiction within this unity reveal the genuine visage of this 'human-God'? It signifies the complete unveiling (which previously became visible in the problem of reality) of the countenance of a profoundly vulnerable 'tragic' human-God—the human-God defined by internal contradiction.

Indeed, it is true: even and especially at this point, it is the case that, for the third and decisive time, the outlines of Thomas Aquinas become visible through the aporetic Kant. However, through the features of the 'doctor communis,' the intricacy of the problem becomes sharper than before. For the sequence of his writings shows us how the otherwise seemingly even-tempered master (in this, our ultimate problem) has seen almost only the problem's different aspects, which are so difficult to reconcile, one after the other. The writings of Aquinas's early period undoubtedly prefer a solution to the problem of individuality that would somewhat correspond to universalism: the individual as more or less a pure 'number' and the 'universal' alone as quality, 'individuum de ratione materiae.' The writings of the late period, on the other hand, tend, increasingly, toward a solution more in line with individualism: the individual as a true, inherent quality[30], and the unity of these many, individual, inherent qualities in God, whose infinity manifests itself precisely in the diversity of this abundance of qualities, 'individuum de ratione formae.' But this is the crucial point where Thomas, especially in this problem, provides the solution against Kant and crowns the solution for philosophy as a whole: his two aspects of the problem

30. *Eigenqualität.*—Trans.

of individuality do not contradict one another because they converge toward the One, the absolute God.

The tension inherent in the expansion of the two aspects just outlined is merely the strongest expression of that primeval tension in which, and from which, Thomas saw the solution to the problem of reality. The first aspect is the 'individuum de ratione materiae,' meaning the individual as a 'numerical instance' of the 'universal,' the individual purely as a member. This aspect of the solution of the problem of reality culminates in the 'Person as Member.' The second aspect is the 'individuum de ratione formae,' meaning the individual as inherent quality, as an individual in itself as a whole. This aspect of the solution to the problem of reality culminates in the 'Person as Whole.' Therefore, in the mysterious intertwining of these two aspects is found the completion of the intertwining, as it emerged in Thomas's solution to the problem of reality: the interplay of 'Person as All' (and therefore 'individuum de ratione formae') and 'Person as Member' (and therefore 'individuum de ratione materiae') as the interplay of God-likeness and God-unlikeness in the *analogia entis*. Through this interplay, the gaze extends to the true God, who, beyond the tension between 'universal' and 'individual,' is personal, all-infinite Fullness, 'Tu solus.' He alone, not some presumptuous 'human-God' of 'humanity,' is God alone as the absolute objective, from which all objectivity of a 'pure universal' on earth is only a faint gleam. He, in His identity with Himself[31], is Personhood absolutely, from which all the original individuality of a 'pure individual' on earth is only a weak intimation.

III

THE AGREEMENT BETWEEN KANT AND THOMAS

So, at first glance, there are certainly specific *correspondences between Kant and Thomas*: in the basic question posed by the

31. *Derselbe als Derselbe.*—Trans.

philosophical situation of their times, as well as in their distinctive epistemological and metaphysical approaches to finding a solution.

*

Regarding the basic question.

Is it true that, based on their relationship to their respective philosophical prehistories and environments, Thomas is the classical pinnacle of 'dogmatic' philosophy, while Kant is the classical pinnacle of 'critical' philosophy? Is Thomas, within the scope of the philosophy of his time, the consummate figure of a philosophy that directly presents the essence of the world without first posing the question of the limits of our knowledge of this essence? Is Kant, within the scope of the philosophy of his time, the consummate figure of a philosophy that poses the question of the limits of knowledge to such an extent that the essence of the world becomes for it only a 'limit concept' for these limits?

Since the publication of Cardinal [Franz] Ehrle's and Martin Grabmann's seminal studies, we know that *Thomas* cannot simply be regarded as a 'Christian Aristotelian,' but that his position (as he himself explains in a passage in the *Disputed Questions*) lies in between two extremes. At the one extreme, there is a philosophy that, in its wide-ranging, almost aesthetically oriented speculations, seems to know next to nothing about 'critique.' Not only does the intricate, concrete world dissolve into a transparent system of thought for it, but this thought system itself is naïvely receptive. Philosophy is an enlightenment from above. In this illumination, the mind beholds pure ideas, and these ideas are the true essence of the world. This Illuminationism and Exemplarism of the early Augustinian schools (this is the philosophical tendency I was referring to above) is therefore 'dogmatic'—i.e., makes uncritical assertions along two lines. First, in the sense of uncritically accepting intellectual experiences: these experiences appear to be immediately inspired by God or are seen in His light and thus are 'dogmatic' not only in the sense of making 'absolute assertions' but also in the sense of making 'assertions about the Absolute (God).' The second sense in which this philosophy is 'dogmatic' is connected to the last one. Because intellectual experiences are 'absolute' in and of themselves and not only in comparison with reality, the second sense of 'critique'—i.e., testing thought against a reality independent of it and (in a certain sense) superior to it—also disappears.

The Aristotelianism of the Parisian Arts Faculty stood at the opposite extreme from the 'dogmatism' of the early Augustinian philosophy. The philosophy of the Arts Faculty went so far in its 'critique' that it even dragged the Church's dogmas before the exclusive tribunal of its critique. (In the process, it aspired to something like a 'religion within the bounds of mere reason'). Operating in the methodological wake that follows all critique—namely, the establishment of ultimate 'antinomies' or points of ultimate incompatibility—this philosophy went so far as to speak, either openly or secretly, of a fundamental antinomy within 'truth itself,' the antinomy of 'double truth' (which holds that what is true in one domain can be false for the other). In doing so, this philosophy anticipated all the antinomies of modern times, whether the typical antinomies of 'pure reason' and 'practical reason,' 'thought' and 'experience,' 'law' and 'value,' 'philosophy' and 'religion.' The existence of this antithesis is a historical fact, and it is equally true that Thomas Aquinas stands between these two extremes as their synthesis. It follows that Aquinas's approach is not an inquiry worked out from within 'dogmatism' but expressly from within the relationship between 'dogmatism' and 'criticism.'

And what of *Kant*? We can see his approach most clearly as a symbol when we consider the two interpretations of it that are diametrically opposed to each other. On the one hand, there is a more or less skeptical-agnostic interpretation, the type of in-terpretation common in the pre-war period.[32] According to this view, Kant is the great demolisher of all 'dogmatism,' ranging from the dogmatism of asserting the reality of things-in-themselves to that of a truth-in-itself. From this perspective, Kant's approach would be purely critical.

On the other hand, this interpretation is sharply opposed to the one that has increasingly come to characterize our post-war era and that finds its strongest expression in Richard Kroner's work, *Von Kant bis Hegel*.[33] Here, Kant appears as the founder of a type of genuinely dogmatic metaphysics—the metaphysics of personal spirit. This metaphysics, in contrast to a metaphysics of objective being, found its fullest expression in Hegel. Thus, Kant's critical approach, for this interpretation, is only the fore-ground expression of the questioning of a new dogmatic meta-physics vis-à-vis an old one. In the final analysis, then, it too is dogmatic.

This antithesis sharply reflects the true stance of the en-igmatic philosopher from Königsberg. On the one hand, he undoubtedly aligns himself with the camp of English skeptics against the overconfident reason of rationalists like Wolff and his school, who carried dogmatism to the extreme of asserting 'first principles' from which the entire richness of the world could be deduced. On the other hand, however, the positive trajec-tory from the *Critique of Pure Reason* to the *Critique of Judg-ment* also undeniably aims at overcoming English skepticism and empiricism, indeed, at overcoming it in such a way that the 'intelligible world,' the 'realm of purposes,' the community of spiritual persons appears as what is 'essential'—that which is given through itself. Kant's fundamental question, therefore, is

32. I.e., before World War I.—Trans.

33. See Richard Kroner, *Von Kant bis Hegel*, 2 vols. (Tübingen, DE: Mohr Siebeck, 1921–24). Vol. 1, *Von der Vernunftkritik zur Naturphilosophie* (1921); vol. 2, *Von der Naturphilosophie zur Philosophie des Geistes* (1924).—Trans.

ultimately situated between criticism and dogmatism and aims at their synthesis. However, doesn't the self-assured rationalism of the Wolffian school renew a feature of the early Augustinianism of 'eternal truths'? And doesn't the criticism and skepticism of the English philosophers reflect the audacity of the philosophers of the Arts Faculty? Consequently, doesn't Kant's attempt at a synthesis resemble Aquinas's in important ways?

*

A path to a solution.

A synthesis between what is genuine in criticism and dogmatism will evidently unite two elements. First (corresponding to criticism), there is the phenomenon of epistemic limits—i.e., our knowledge's bond to experience and thereby its limits regarding what is beyond experience. However, second (pertaining to dogmatism), there is the primacy of the spiritual in our knowledge beyond the sub-spiritual nature of the purely known. If the first element turns into a critical epistemology, then the second becomes a metaphysics of the spiritual-intelligible. In both, there appears to be a similarity between Thomas and Kant.

In epistemology.

First, both Thomas and Kant place the starting point of philosophy in thought's reflection on itself. In his main epistemological treatise, the *Quaestiones disputatae de Veritate*, Thomas calls for a 'reflexio' of the intellect upon itself, primarily focusing on its formal act, and it is in this that truth is grounded.[34] Kant poses a similar fundamental question. For his question "How are synthetic a priori judgments possible?" addresses the formal nature of human thinking, which is both bound to experience ('synthetic judgments') and transcends the factual-empirical realm of experience to reach the timeless, necessary nature of the ideal ('a priori judgments').

34. Thomas Aquinas, *De Veritate* 1.9.

47

Second, both Thomas and Kant view the significance of thinking, insofar as it pursues truth, decidedly not in an intuition of ideas[35] but in the formal act of judgment. For Thomas, truth does not formally reside in the essence-intuiting thought of the 'intellectus formans quidditates' but in the analyzing and synthesizing activity of the 'intellectus dividens et componens.' It is not found in 'apprehensio' but in 'iudicium,' not in the receptive 'intellectus possibilis' but in the spontaneous 'intellectus agens.' In stark contrast to the ideational speculation of rationalism, Kant emphasizes the act of judgment and, thus, conceives of his categories as forms of judgment. Thinking qua thinking is spontaneity.

Third, both Thomas and Kant emphasize, against an unrestrained flight of ideas (whether in early Augustinianism or German rationalism), the tethering and limitation of human thought by sensory experience. Thomas underscores in his philosophy of science, as articulated in the commentary on Boethius's *De Trinitate*, that fundamentally the 'principia prima'—which early Augustinianism assumed to be immediately intuited—are 'ex sensibilibus,' derived from and intertwined with sensory experience (though not exclusively so). He further contends that we can only apprehend everything that is purely spiritual ultimately in its existence (*quod sit*), not in its essential being (*quid sit*), resulting in our knowledge of it being fundamentally negative (knowing what it is not). Thus, our knowledge of God culminates in acknowledging God 'tamquam ignotum,' as the 'unknown God.' Even the knowledge derived from revelation fundamentally alters nothing in this regard—it may expand the circle of objects known but does not relinquish the 'modus' of sensory knowledge. Kant intertwines sensory experience and categorical thinking so closely that experience without thought is blind. However, thought without experience is empty, and consequently, while the

35. *Inhalten.*—Trans.

existence of a transcendent world cannot be denied, it can only be recognized in the form of 'limit ideas,' meaning it cannot be positively known in itself.

In metaphysics.

An epistemology that places its emphasis on the formal act of knowing and—based on consideration of its nature as act, either intentionally in Thomas or categorically in Kant—turns toward the world of objects evidently emphasizes the 'world in knowledge.' It focuses on the world as it stands out in the act of abstracting (Thomas) or categorizing (Kant), presenting it as the 'essential world' in contrast to the factual-empirical sensory world. Such an epistemology logically evolves into a metaphysics of such an 'essential' world. It gives rise to a metaphysics of the 'intelligible.'

It is characteristic of Thomas's thought that the two constituents of the factual-empirical sensory world—namely, space and time—belong to the 'materia' that, for him, is 'pura potentialitas,' i.e., the changeable aspect of the world of 'formae,' which alone 'truly exists.' This is how his worldview appears when we consider it, for instance, in *De Ente et Essentia* and in the disputed questions *De Spiritualibus Creaturis*—namely, as an image of a structure of 'intelligible forms' that, so to speak, 'materializes' from above. This structure hovers between the 'pure intelligibility' of pure spirits (each of which is a 'species' exempt from spatio-temporal individualization) and the 'formae materiales' of natural bodies that are inherently spatio-temporal. So, it is no wonder that in *De Veritate*, Thomas tends to attribute intrinsic intelligibility to being in general, considering 'knowability' as an intrinsic quality perceived by the act of 'knowing' itself. For everything that in any sense 'is,' is such by virtue of the 'actual being' of the intelligible 'forma.'

However, Kant's metaphysics (as recently elucidated by [Heinz] Heimsoeth's research) is directed against Spinoza's metaphysics of space and time, which appeared to him as the materialization of the mind. Therefore, his critique of the proofs of God consistently targets those based on the spatio-temporal world, and he treats the teleological argument—which takes the specifically intellectual phenomenon of purposiveness as its starting point—with comparative gentleness. Kant accentuates the 'Deus in nobis,' the spontaneity of thinking and willing. So, it is only logical that his three critiques increasingly redefine metaphysics as an 'intelligible world' or a 'realm of purposes.' His de-objectification of space and time takes on a new aspect, a Platonic-Aristotelian aspect, asserting that the spatio-temporal sensory world 'essentially is not' because only the intellectual realm of essential forms 'essentially is.'

Does it not indeed seem that there is a surprising similarity between large parts of the philosophy of Thomas Aquinas and the philosophy of Kant? Is the opposition that exists between them, according to the traditional view, merely an illusion?

IV

THE FUNDAMENTAL OPPOSITION BETWEEN
KANT AND THOMAS

However, the *fundamental opposition between Kant and Thomas* resides precisely in those points where agreement seemed to us to prevail.

It is initially a fundamental opposition between what one could call the *inner ethos* of their philosophies. If we open Aquinas's *Quaestiones disputatae* or, even more so, the first parts of his *Summa Theologiae*, a breath of almost marble-like, calm objectivity wafts toward us. It is as if an eye calmly opened to reality gazes back at us. It is a language that does not exaggerate anything. It is a course of inquiry that, seemingly indifferent to strict logical progression, meanders freely to the right and left, unfolding contemplatively yet unconsciously bearing crystalline unity within itself. It is a philosophy that stands before clear results and dark mysteries with equal calmness and detachment, speaking with the same serene measure about the abundance of God's attributes as it does about the recognition that He is ultimately known 'tamquam ignotus,' as the solemn enigma of all creaturely thought.

When we compare this to Kant, his announcement of a reversal in philosophizing sounds idiosyncratic from the outset. His spirit almost defiantly turns away from a disruptive chaotic environment, insisting that the latter must be shaped according to the blueprints of solitary thought before one can trust it. He audaciously forces a world of perception spanning centuries into his compass at any cost, right up to the unbearable construal of the religious world in his *Religion within the Boundaries of Mere Reason*. His boundary-setting 'No' resonates sharply when he touches upon the great mysteries of existence—not with calm reverence for their veiled nature and a serene gaze into them but turning away from them as inconvenient boundaries to thought's omnipotence in the realm where it rules undisturbed. The proud declaration of the will's autonomy and the gloom of radical evil—deification and demonization of the creaturely—starkly intersect in Kant's thought!

Now, Thomas's measured approach and Kant's exclusivity also influence their respective philosophies. Why, then, when Thomas takes an epistemological approach and begins with the subject does it lead to an *epistemological metaphysics* of the relationship of the receiving creature—together with other co-receiving [creatures]—to the giving God[36], and thus to an epistemological metaphysics of cognition that has been internally and humanely redeemed, that integrates itself as a part into, or, better said, knows itself integrated into an existing world full of meaning? And why, then, when Kant takes an epistemological approach and begins with the subject does it result in such a confinement of

---

36. *empfangenden Geschöpfes mit mit-empfangenden zum schenkenden Gott.*—Trans.

the All within the subject that it now splits into two sharply op-posing spheres—the upper one being a 'pure subjectivity,' where the knowing self becomes the It of objectivity, and the lower one being an 'empirical subjectivity,' where the same self bears the inescapable curse of an unbridgeable distance to itself as 'pure subjectivity'? Why, further, does the *metaphysics of an intelligible world* in Thomas manifest as one where the sensory world and the intelligible world—the realm of 'pure matter' and the realm of 'intelligible forms'—harmoniously resonate, creating something like their inner center in humans: in the 'anima forma corpo-ris,' the body animated by the soul and the soul enfleshed in the body? And why does the metaphysics of an intelligible world in Kant reveal itself in the stark contours of the unresolved con-tradiction between a realm of spirit, which is denied to human thought as such, and a realm of the senses, which is essentially chaos and nonbeing, while the postulate of reconciliation (the Leibnizian residue!) shifts into the elusive realm of limit ideas?

We see the answer to these questions when we gaze into the *religious countenance* of both thinkers. From *Kant's* face, the unrec-onciled antithesis of two forms of religiosity confronts us, whose struggle against each other characterizes the Enlightenment era. The first is the Reformation religiosity of 'God alone'—sovereign in condemnation and mono-causal bestowal of grace—who so towers over creation that the creaturely nature appears inherently sinful and human reason is called 'whore reason.' The second form of religiosity is the Enlightenment piety of 'Deus in nobis,' 'God in us,' which finds expression in the all-creative human reason, next to which God, the sovereign ruler, is only the divine luster of the solely divine 'pure reason.' But a terrible connection exists between the two: the second piety is fundamentally the child of the first, carrying its mortal enemy in its womb. For when, in the Reformational experience of salvation, God and the human are so inseparable that God is the sole actor within the human being, are not the outlines of a doctrine already taking shape—one that calls the ideally human 'God' and the empirically sinful human 'creature,' God within humans as 'Humanity'? So, is the intertwining of contradictions, as we perceive it in the innermost face of Kant's philosophy, not the straightforward consequence of the profound connection in its underlying religiosity: the devotee of Humanity[37] who cannot break free from Lutheranism, and the Lutheran who reluctantly begets the devotee of Humanity?

But then, the measure and harmony of the philosophy of *Thomas Aquinas* also reveals its opposing religious countenance. It is a piety that does not demand the assurance of an ascertainable closeness to God but calmly and selflessly places the I in the hands of a God who is not there to be a means of salvation for humans. Instead, 'praise, reverence, and service' of Him constitute the meaning of the world, an immersion in the radiance of His Majesty. However, it is also a piety that—precisely because of this reverence and devotion to a truly transcendent God—gently gazes upon His creation as the individually differentiated abundance of His inexhaustible infinity. In this sense of the 'manifestatio perfectionis divinae,' it skillfully integrates even the mysteries and obscurities of this creation. For no tormenting anxiety about a most assured 'rescue from this world' clouds Thomas's objectivity. Surrendered to God's 'unfathomable counsels,' he gazes from the eternally tranquil God into the world. This is the decisive reason why Thomas is both the philosopher of the decisive transcendence of God and, at the same time, the philosopher of the 'causa secunda'—i.e., proper causal agency of creatures[38]. Indeed, he derives their proper causal agency[39] and proper worth directly from the transcendence of God. As he puts it: "God's fullness consists in the fact that He can communicate His own being."

Thus, the decisive difference between Thomas and Kant is

37. *der Humanitätsfromme.*—Trans.
38. *Eigenwirklichkeit.*—Trans.
39. *Eigenwirksamkeit.*—Trans.

this: with Kant, we have a philosophy born of anxious construction from a piety of anxious certainty about salvation, whereas with Thomas, we have a philosophy born of liberated openness to the diversity and change in things, stemming from a piety of selfless devotion to God's infinite and incomprehensible majesty.

3

From Kant to Thomas

The comparative study we have just completed raises of itself the pivotal question that must guide our whole investigation: To what extent is it possible to break through to Thomas from the dilemma immanent to Kant? We can address this question in two ways: negatively, in response to the attempts that have already been made in this direction, and positively, in outlining the possible ways. Here, we are drawn more deeply than before into the fundamental questions of [1] apriorism, [2] transcendentalism, and [3] metaphysics. The following three sections will be structured accordingly. The question of apriorism will be presented by engaging with Maréchal, who introduces his 'transposition' between Thomas and Kant in this context. We can proceed more positively with the questions about transcendentalism and metaphysics. However, our port of entry into the latter will be the confrontation between Heidegger's and Herrigel's views on Kant.

Our investigation leads down this path to something that has been unfolding from the very beginning: a positive foundation for philosophy as a metaphysics of the *analogia entis*.

I

APRIORISM

At present, the problem of *apriorism* is found in a kind of convergence between Kantian-oriented philosophy and Scholastic philosophy. In the former, it is found in the way Husserl's questioning delved ever deeper and compelled scholars in the humanities (Rothacker) and natural sciences (Dingler)[1] to confront the

---

1. Erich Rothacker and Hugo Dingler.—Trans.

question of the hidden, a priori assumptions of their methodology. For neo-scholasticism, the problem can be seen, first and
foremost, in French-Belgian neo-Thomism's turning away from
the earlier, more inductive metaphysical style of the schools in
Belgium (Mercier) and Germany (Gutberlet and Geyser).[2] Thus,
the question naturally arises, as posed by Maréchal,[3] about the
internal relationship between a Kantian and Thomistic apriorism.

Maréchal begins with a *critical examination of the possibilities.*
This examination naturally extends first to the determination of
the historical formulation of both Thomas's and Kant's questions
and then to the possibility of a common denominator for both.

With *Thomas*, he sees very soberly the significant challenge
inherent in studying Aquinas's philosophy: its basically theological orientation. [Alexandre] Koyré coined the rather apt term
'religious metaphysics' for this type of Scholastic summa.

St. Thomas did not write an epistemology [*épistémologie*];[4] he
did not even publish a systematic exposition of his philosophy.
The *Summa contra Gentiles*, sometimes called the *Summa
philosophica*, is above all a treatise on religious apologetics.
The *Quaestiones disputatae* touch on a number of questions
of pure philosophy. In the *Commentary on the Sentences* and
in the *Summa Theologica*, his philosophical thought, though
alive throughout, adapts and restrains its manifestations to the
framework of dogmatic teaching. Remaining, as works of pure

2. Désiré Mercier, Constantin Gutberlet, and Joseph Geyser.—Trans.

3. Joseph Maréchal, *Le point de départ de la Métaphysique: Leçons sur le développement historique et théorique du problème de la connaissance,* 4 vols. (Bruges, BE: Beyaert, 1922–26). Vol.
1, *De l'antiquité à la fin du moyen âge: La critique ancienne de la connaisance* (1922); vol. 2, *Le
conflit du Rationalisme et de l'Empirisme dans la philosophie moderne, avant Kant* (1923); vol. 3,
La Critique de Kant (1923); vol. 5, *Le Thomisme devant la Philosophie critique* (1926). The prom-
ised fourth volume was assembled from his writings and published posthumously as *Le point
de départ de la Métaphysique: Leçons sur le développement historique et théorique du problème de
la connaissance,* vol. 4, *Le système idéaliste chez Kant et les postkantiens* (Brussels, BE: Universelle;
Paris: Desclée du Brouwer, 1947). A proposed sixth volume, *Les épistémologies contemporaines,*
was never published.—Trans.

4. 'Épistémologie' is the term of the modern French and Belgian Scholastic schools for the
critique of knowledge (*epistēmē*).

philosophy, are the commentaries on Aristotle and a certain number of particular *Opuscula*.[5]

With *Kant*, the difficulty arises from the various lines of thought that, despite their opposition, all invoke him. Therefore, in his volume on Kant,[6] Maréchal chooses to reduce the issue to Kant's immediate question as it emerged from his historical situation. The result is the image of a Kant who 'brackets.' That is, the image of a Kant who makes any absolute assertions about the essence of the world completely recedes in favor of a Kant committed solely to the methodological approach of 'this far I come with my critique,' which, in comparison with everything else, implies neither affirmation nor negation.

> The transcendental method of analyzing the object is a precise and non-exclusive method. In the object of spontaneous knowledge, it only considers the immediate influence of the faculties that constitute it as a known object. In Kantian terms, it examines the constitutive a priori of the object—or, in other words, the transcendental conditions of the object's possibility (in contrast to its empirical condition, the sensory datum). In Scholastic language, this means that it contemplates the knowable in act according to the conditions that constitute it in its knowable actuality—or, in simpler terms, that the knowable in act is identically the knowing in act—or, yet again, according to the functional priority (a limited aspect of metaphysical priority) of the knowing faculties over their objective operations.[7]

In this way, Maréchal not only gives a positive sense to the doctrine of a priori forms[8] but also thinks he can justify the

5. Maréchal, *Métaphysique*, 5:34.
6. Maréchal, *Métaphysique*, vol. 3.
7. Maréchal, 5:32.
8. Maréchal, 3:93–145.

famous 'Copernican revolution' to some extent. This is because the 'lawgiver of nature' refers only to phenomena and not to the things-in-themselves.[9] Thus, he primarily works his way through Kant's aporetic questioning:

> It is nevertheless true that Kant had, as early as 1772, grasped and formulated the central problem of the *Critique of Pure Reason*: how are objects possible in thought? Or, if one prefers, what are the conditions of possibility for objective thought? To be objective is to have a relation to the object. . . . Our pure concepts could only contract this relation in two ways: a) as products of the object received in the subject; but then they would no longer be pure, a priori concepts but particular representations of passive, empirical, and therefore sensory data: a passive representation as intellectual is an absurdity; or b) as productive causes of the object: but it is obvious that our intelligence does not create the object to which it refers: an active intellectual intuition that totally produces its object, even if it were possible, is beyond the reach of human understanding.[10]

The final judgment on Kant (despite every rejection of the pure theories of limit ideas[11]) is the question of whether it might not be possible "to force Kant to surpass himself, to deny, in the name of his *Critique*, the agnostic conclusions of his *Critique*."[12] Maréchal's answer is that the "epistemological principles" of Thomism could "enlarge" the "masterful but incomplete analyses of Kant."[13]

Maréchal begins by *distinguishing between two types of epistemologies*. The first type subordinates knowledge to being and

9. Maréchal, 3:152f.
10. Maréchal, 3:56f.
11. Maréchal, 3:192ff., 206ff.
12. Maréchal, 3:239.
13. Maréchal, 3:239.

seeks to justify the objectivity of knowledge through a reduction to ontological issues (according to Maréchal, primarily focusing on the problem of unity and multiplicity[14]): a "metaphysical critique of the object." The second type considers knowledge in its distinct nature as an immanent act of the subject and seeks to demonstrate the objectivity of knowledge by reducing it to the pure properties of the act. These properties, in their formality, uniformly correspond to the material aspects of various objects: a "transcendental critique of the object."[15]

The first type is characteristic of ancient and medieval epistemology.

> They perceived very early on that the mind's raw contents contain contradictory elements, which cannot indiscriminately be the object of legitimate affirmations; the problem boiled down to introducing, in the mind's contents, the necessary distinctions and gradations to safeguard the first normative principle while also accommodating the absolute and universal necessity of affirmation.[16]

The second type is Kant's. Maréchal understands 'transcendental' here in the general sense of the formality of the faculty of knowledge ("a radical critique of the very faculty of knowing"[17]), thus essentially taking the word in its negative sense as the antithesis to 'transcendent' (in the sense of the 'things in themselves'). He practically adopts the methodological standpoint of ordinary neo-scholastic epistemology, which designates the problem of knowledge as the 'bridge' problem[18]—i.e., the problem of the relationship between the immanent world of consciousness and

---

14. Maréchal, 1:13, 153; 2:viii, etc.
15. Maréchal, 5:13.
16. Maréchal, 5:13.
17. Maréchal, 5:13.
18. *Problem "de ponte."*—Trans.

reality.[19] The deeper discussion of the concept 'transcendental' in its positive sense—whether 'transcendental' in terms of the anthropological ideality of the 'subject in itself' (as the antithesis to the empirical subject) or voluntaristic positing (as an antithesis to passive experiencing) or pure validity (as the antithesis to the empirical phenomenon)—is left out of consideration for the confrontation between Thomas and Kant. In practice, Maréchal only restricts the epistemological object to the 'metaphysical affirmation' (unfortunately, he does not elaborate on this anywhere). In other words, he takes the object of epistemology to be (at least decisively) not the knowledge of practical sensory reality in the empirical sciences, but intelligible reality in pure metaphysics. The object is not the reality of the individual world but the reality of the world of essences. Yet, it is not this object insofar as it may be conceived as something 'in itself' but as it is the 'true' world 'in' the world. For Maréchal, the two questions that we have learned to sharply distinguish since Husserl—the question about essences and the question about reality—are a single, identical question.

With this terminology, Maréchal now envisions a *twofold possible relationship between the two types*. First, there is the possibility of reducing the transcendental (in Maréchal's sense) to the metaphysical type. In this sense, Maréchal speaks of a historically actual "interpenetration of metaphysics and epistemology" in the direction of the "problem of unity and multiplicity" in antiquity and the Middle Ages[20] as well as of a "restoration of the necessary unity of the one and the many" in Kant's critique, thus indicating the ultimate, metaphysical character of his transcendentalism.[21] The second possible relation is that of a 'transposition' of the metaphysical type onto the transcendental. Unlike the first possibility, which is purely historical, this is a neglected option and the real object of Maréchal's investigation. The fifth volume, titled *Le*

19. Maréchal, 3:79; 5:393, among others.
20. Maréchal, 2:vii.
21. Maréchal, 3:ix.

Thomisme devant la Philosophie critique, culminates in presenting Thomistic metaphysical epistemology[22] not only in the language of transcendental epistemology but also in demonstrating that what he has just presented serves as the internal fulfillment and solution to the historical, transcendental type.[23] Thus, Maréchal's exposition of the preconditions directly merges into his presentation of the problem.

*

The *problem* posed by Maréchal of internally embracing the demands of Kant's philosophy ("to challenge the absolute and universal legitimacy, if not the relative opportunity, of the methodological demands of Kantianism"[24]) and his subsequent effort to internally overcome its de facto agnosticism through Thomas or the Thomism he delineates ("to broaden Kant's masterful but incomplete analyses"[25])—this problem indeed naturally arises from the terminological and historical foundations just outlined.

First, the limitation *to the justification of the 'metaphysical affirmation'* leads Maréchal to place Thomism and Kantianism on the common ground of examining an object that, according to both, is not real in its formal structure—for neither Kantianism nor Thomism considers the 'universal' as an absolutely existing reality. Thomas expresses this idea with the distinction between 'id quod' (the content of a 'universal,' for example, what belongs to the essence of humanity in general) and 'modus quo' (the form of universality, for example, the essence of 'human in itself'). What exist in reality are always individual human beings, and in that sense, the 'human in itself' does not belong to the realm of reality but is a product of thought. But the humans that exist in reality are indeed 'humans,' and in this regard, the 'human in

22. Maréchal, 5:33–384.
23. Maréchal, 5:385–461.
24. Maréchal, 5:viii.
25. Maréchal, 3:239.

61

itself' is not a fiction. This is expressed in Kant's terms through the distinction between the necessary and the purely factual. I know the necessary in its material content only in connection with the purely factual (the 'essence' human only in connection with the sensory experiences of given individual humans). Still, I do not encounter it 'qua' necessary in the purely factual. The necessary 'qua' necessary (the Thomistic *forma universalitatis*) is thus 'a priori,' but according to its concrete content (the Thomistic *materia universalitatis*), 'a posteriori.' Consequently, the comprehensive knowledge of the necessary is 'synthetic,' and since the necessary, under the aspect of the 'form' of necessity, is what is decisive, it is 'synthetic a priori,' meaning a synthesis of 'a priori' and 'a posteriori,' in which the 'a priori' constitutes the formal element.

The common ground now expands—second—through the *methodological equation* that Maréchal establishes between the *problem of unity and multiplicity* as the core of metaphysics and the *problem of intellect and sensory knowledge* as the core of epistemology. This results in a theory that unites the metaphysical and transcendental types of epistemologies, presenting itself as a "theory of the synthetic concept that is made multiplicable by extrinsic relation to quantity, yet unified under the unlimited unity of being."[26] That is, in the knowledge of the real-metaphysical (in the sense in which we explained it earlier), there is an intellectual unification between the more passively receptive sensory knowledge prompted by the external sensory world and the intellectual knowledge that processes the sensory elements. In Thomas, this synthesis takes place through the 'intellectus agens,' while in Kant, it is facilitated by the 'a priori categories' as manifestations of 'spontaneity.' This unification occurs between the sensory external world as the 'world of multiplicity' and that principle of unity, which only becomes evident

26. Maréchal, 5:40.

in intellectual knowledge (whether conceived as a self-contained act in Kant, or as aiming at 'pure being' in an 'assimilative-final' manner[27], as Maréchal puts it, in Thomas). As Maréchal repeatedly emphasizes, this equation finds its ultimate expression in the equivalence between the Thomistic metaphysical principle of act-potency and the Kantian transcendental (in Maréchal's sense) principle of spontaneity-receptivity.

Knowledge in general, according to Maréchal, is characterized by the relationship between the object-conditioned 'id quod' of the concrete content of knowledge and the subject-conditioned 'modus quo' of the mode of the cognitive act,[28] signifying a relationship whereby the 'id quod' is shaped by the 'modus quo.'[29] This shaping occurs within pure sensory knowledge only imperfectly, although still in a certain true sense,[30] and reaches its zenith in intellectual knowledge, from the shaping 'intellectus agens' of humans to the purely 'a priori' knowledge of angels.[31] For it is epistemically true that "immanence is the condition and measure of knowledge."[32] This fact is expressed initially in general terms: in Thomistic metaphysical language as the fact of 'actus immanens' and in Kantian transcendental language as the 'self-contained character of consciousness'[33]. In light of the fundamental principles of the two systems given above, it means that, for the Thomistic metaphysical type, 'act' is the formal principle of 'potency,' and for the Kantian transcendentalist type, 'spontaneity' is the formal principle of 'receptivity.' In Thomism, 'potency' serves as the principle of multiplicity, while 'act' serves as the principle of unity. Similarly, in Kantian transcendentalism, 'spontaneity' functions as the principle establishing

27. *assimilatorisch-final.*—Trans.
28. Maréchal, 1:45, 66ff., among others.
29. Maréchal, 1:66ff.
30. Maréchal, 3:99ff.
31. Maréchal, 5:95ff., 103ff.
32. Maréchal, 5:70.
33. *Bewußtseinsgeschlossenheit.*—Trans.

unity[34], while 'receptivity' serves as the principle for experiencing multiplicity[35]. However, in Thomism, act and potency are one as the singular metaphysical 'becoming.' Spontaneity and receptivity in Kant are one as the singular transcendental movement of consciousness[36] ("the *fieri* of the immanent object"[37]). The equation between unity-multiplicity and intellectual-sensory knowledge thus traces back to the equation between act-potency and spontaneity-receptivity. This, in turn, is the expression of the equation between metaphysical 'becoming' and transcendental 'becoming.' The age-old problem of becoming, solved in terms of act and potency, is, therefore, the crucial commonality between Thomas and Kant.

Third, a final problem thus decisively and conclusively moves to the forefront in this whole problematic: the *problem of finality*. For everything that is moved-becoming[38] is somehow directed toward a goal by its internal constitution. Therefore, if the act of knowing, according to both Thomas and Kant, is a moved-becoming, it follows that its inner meaning is decisively manifested in its practical orientation toward a goal. The characteristic by which the act of knowing is termed an 'action' serves as evidence of whether it (transcendentally) rests within itself (and so is not only considered methodologically-transcendentally within itself but is also held to be systematically-transcendentally self-contained) or (metaphysically) aims at objective being.

Here we are at the apex of Maréchal's problem. For it is here that both the ultimate commonality between Thomas and Kant unfolds, as well as their decisive opposition.

Their ultimate *commonality*.

According to Maréchal, the proof of the objectivity of knowing

34. *Einheitsetzung.*—Trans.
35. *Vielheiterfahrung.*—Trans.
36. *Bewußtseins-Bewegtsein.*—Trans.
37. Maréchal, 5:29.
38. *Werdend-Bewegte.*—Trans.

for both Thomas and Kant—breaking through, in Thomistic terms, from the 'species' to the 'res,' or in Kantian terms, from the 'phenomena' to the 'things in themselves'—resides in its active nature. Thus, for Thomas, it resides in cognition's inner 'appetitus naturalis' for 'Being' and the 'Good' that corresponds to it,[39] and for Kant, it resides in 'practical reason.' Maréchal brings both perspectives together in the common formula: "the objective value of knowledge" is "formally manifested to the subject through the analysis of its own a priori requirements."[40] However, this 'action-finality,' in the same way for both Thomas and Kant, terminates in the 'last end'—i.e., in God. It does so either, in the case of Kant, as the limit concept of the 'transcendental ideal'—i.e., the itself unconditioned but all-conditioning condition of 'all possibility' for objects.[41] Or, in the case of Thomas, it is understood as the 'ipsum esse,' the 'pure Being' that, as the primal ground of all being, is the ultimate meaning of every movement of the intellect, as the 'actus purus' and the primal foundation of all its 'action.'[42] Thomas and Kant are, according to Maréchal, united in an '*a priori objectivism*'—i.e., in an interpretation of the a priori character of knowledge that does not deny the objectivity of knowledge but rather asserts its possibility.[43] Second, they are united in a '*final dynamism*'—i.e., in an actual justification of knowledge's intrinsic claim to objectivity arising from the practical, goal-oriented movement of the act of knowing.[44]

Their decisive *opposition*.

For in Kant, the consideration of the active character of knowing leads only to the 'postulates' of practical reason—i.e.,

39. Maréchal, 5:263–306.
40. Maréchal, 5:374.
41. Maréchal, 3:190ff.
42. Maréchal, 5:333–69.
43. Maréchal, 5:103ff.
44. Maréchal, 3:237ff.; 5:33ff.

only to a "moral or practical necessity,"[45] and so to one that does not eliminate the agnosticism of theoretical reason.[46] For Thomas, however, the 'appetitus naturalis' of knowing toward 'Being' becomes not only a postulate upon which knowing's true objectivity is founded (by virtue of the axiom 'desiderium naturale non potest esse frustaneum'[47]). It further establishes a "theoretical necessity"[48] of objectivity through an "analytical demonstration, highlighting the link of dependence that exists between the rational coherence of the tendency and the ontological possibility of the End ['Being in itself']. This occurs in such a way that, where the logical incoherence of the tendency is not admissible, the ontological possibility of the End is absolutely necessary."[49] Logically, this opposition reaches its apex in the understanding of the 'last end' that gives this striving its character.

In Kant, the 'ens realissimum,' i.e., God, in theoretical reason only possesses the character of a limit concept, the 'ultimate condition' for all 'conditions of knowledge' (thus, it is a "negative noumenon," as Maréchal aptly puts it, "a non-phenomenon, at most, a problematic reality in the unknowable sphere of pure intelligibles"[50]). Practical reason's postulate of God shares the character of all its postulates, which, despite the teleological principle of the *Critique of Judgment*, "remain subjective and relative"[51]—i.e., they do not allow for a theoretical justification of the reality of God.

For Thomas, however, God is substantiated as the 'pure Being' ('ipsum esse'), in which all being originates, precisely in knowledge's internal orientation toward 'Being in itself.' God is thus "implicitly affirmed, as (positive noumenon), in every judgment."

---

45. Maréchal, 1:ix.
46. Maréchal, 3:207, 233–35.
47. natural desire cannot be in vain.—Trans.
48. Maréchal, *Métaphysique*, 1:ix.
49. Maréchal, 5:334.
50. Maréchal, 5:448.
51. Maréchal, 3:235.

This correlates with Kant, for whom the 'negative noumenon' serves as the ultimate regulative idea of every judgment.[52]

However, with this, the treatment of the problem has already imperceptibly transitioned into a treatment of Maréchal's positive thesis.

*

In keeping with the critical examination of the possibilities and the problem, Maréchal's *positive thesis* has two main parts. First, a historical-methodological part that assesses the actual relationship between Thomas and Kant. Second, an objective-methodological[53] part that constructs a specific unity out of this relationship. However, in keeping with our findings above, both main parts address the relationship between Thomas and Kant in terms of their commonalities and their opposition.

First: the historical-methodological relationship.

In short, this relationship consists in the fact that methodological transcendentalism (in Maréchal's sense explained above) is common to both Thomas and Kant. But they fundamentally differ in the ultimate systematic orientation of this transcendentalism. Methodological transcendentalism includes, as its components: first, universal methodical doubt as a starting point; second, a priori objectivism as a theory of the nature of knowledge; and third, final dynamism as a way to justify its claim to objectivity. However, all three components are internally shaped by a systematic transcendentalism, which, for Thomas, is a transcendentalism of being, whereas, for Kant, it is a transcendentalism of the I.

This is expressed first in '*universal methodical doubt.*'

Contrary to the thesis of our new Rhineland Thomism,[54]

---

52. Maréchal, 5:448.

53. *sachmethodischen.*—Trans.

54. Karl Eschweiler, *Die zwei Wege der neueren Theologie: Georg Hermes–Matth. Jos. Scheeben: Eine kritische Untersuchung des Problems der theologischen Erkenntnis* (Augsburg, DE: Benno Filser, 1926), 125ff., among others.

Maréchal demonstrates that Thomas, just like Descartes and Kant, placed the "universalis dubitatio de veritate" at the beginning: "Illi qui volunt inquirere veritatem non considerando prius dubitationem, assimilantur iis qui nesciunt quo vadant. . . . Ista scientia [metaphysica] sicut habet universalem considerationem de veritate, ita etiam ad eam pertinet universalis dubitatio de veritate."[55] But even this initial approach to philosophy, or rather its presupposition, is internally shaped by the contrast between the transcendentalism of being (Thomas), in which the (transcendental) act of knowing aims at (metaphysical) being, and the transcendentalism of the I (Kant), in which it closes in on itself (in transcendental subjectivity).

Descartes endeavors to doubt as much as he can—that is, as strongly and as far as the immediate possibility of doubt extends—without bothering much to assess the intrinsic value of his reasons for doubting. His goal is to reach, with a leap, the solid rock of a self-evident truth: evident enough to appear indubitable from all perspectives and to serve as a solid foundation for the reconstruction of a philosophy. In the case of Aristotle and St. Thomas, methodical doubt is also the questioning, before reflective reason, of the object from which one claims to acquire scientific knowledge. Through a methodological fiction, one temporarily refrains from giving any assent to this object: it is treated "ad modum quaestionis solvendae"; one inquires into the pros and cons, weighs the reasons that seem to argue for or against its value. This attitude is, moreover, here more exclusively negative and expectant than in Descartes; it does not require an artificial effort to doubt positively but only the impartial reserve suitable for the

---

55. Those who wish to inquire into the truth without first considering doubt are like those who do not know where they are going. . . . Just as the universal consideration of truth belongs to this science [metaphysics], so too does universal doubt about truth pertain to it. (Thomas Aquinas, *Commentary on Aristotle's "Metaphysics"* 3.1)—Trans.

objective examination of a cause. It is less a doubt, to be precise, than a momentary suspension of judgment to allow for the consideration of the hypothesis of doubt: "considerando dubitationem." If the appeal to the tribunal of reflection temporarily suspends all prerogatives of spontaneous reason, these prerogatives will be recognized without cavil as soon as their validity becomes apparent. St. Thomas doubts less seriously than Descartes; on the other hand, he doubts more universally, and this matters more. The aim of St. Thomas is not, like that of Descartes, to seize as soon as possible, among other possible 'truths,' a privileged, indubitable, and well-defined truth that can serve as a constructive starting point. His purpose, less particularized, offers more real scope and, pardon the paradox, more fundamental 'modernity': because it is nothing less than instituting a general critique of truth as such. Therefore, the initial results obtained by the method of methodical doubt will be different in Thomism and in Cartesian metaphysics: with the latter, the intuitive evidence of the ontological Self (might one not find oneself imprisoned there?); with the former, the objective necessity of Being in general.[56]

However, in its departure from Descartes, Kant's transcendentalism is directed toward the I[57] and thus toward an 'evidence before the I through the I,' its inner form now being determined by its decisive difference from Thomistic transcendentalism. According to Maréchal (as we saw above), what is common to both Thomas and Kant is one such methodological transcendentalism, which, first, in its intention, is directed toward the explanation and justification of the objectivity of knowledge ('a priori objectivism'), and second, seeks this justification in the finality of the act of knowing ('final dynamism'). The decisive difference between

56. Maréchal, *Métaphysique*, 5:40.
57. The I in Kant only becomes the I of the 'synthetic unity of apperception' from Descartes' more or less 'ontological' I.

Thomas and Kant, according to this interpretation of their commonality, lies in their different manners of justification. Indeed, in Kant, there are the beginnings of a fully developed justification of objectivity based on the finality of the act of knowing. We can find it, first, in the postulates of 'practical reason,' as we have seen. Then, second, [we see a justification of objectivity] in the peculiar role that aesthetics plays in Kant, insofar as the aesthetic judgment reveals not only a "subjective finalism" of the act toward the object in itself—"the harmony of the object with the free, unconstrained play of our faculties"[58]—but also a certain "objective finalism."[59] However, it remains the case that ultimately only the postulates of practical reason pertain to the objective in the sense of the 'things in themselves' and thus (according to what was explained earlier) the fundamental agnosticism of theoretical reason is not abolished.

> The aesthetic feeling appears in us as the natural and immediate 'reactive' response to the teleological exercise of the faculty of judgment: under the aesthetic affirmation—'that is beautiful'—the sentiment that underlies it involves the confused approval of our entire being, which unfolds freely according to its own law. In a very strict sense, one could say that we directly feel our personal finality, and that the finality of objects is a logical postulate of our affective life. As much as the sentiment is valued as a revelation of the depths of our being, so do the theoretical presuppositions of the sentiment—namely, universal finality—hold value. However, let us not exaggerate here either, and let us not subtly slide from Kant to Schleiermacher. The distance remains significant between Kant's postulates of pure practical reason and the presuppositions of the affective life: the former participate in the universal demand of duty, touching the objective and the absolute; the latter are linked to

58. Maréchal, 5:228ff.
59. Maréchal, 5:230ff.

the concrete exercise of a tendency, they remain subjective and relative, no matter how imperative they may be. . . .

Do not forget that, in Kant's own view, the transcendental ideas, being mere subjective requirements of theoretical reason, receive a precious consecration from moral will and sentiment. Through a true convergence of his cognitive and appetitive faculties, man is led from all sides to the affirmation of the same problematic objects: first, God, either as the Absolute Being or, at least, as the 'supreme Architect of the universe'; then the Self, as a moral subject, free and subsistent, or as an active finality reacting to objects; finally, Nature, as a world unity or as a system of objective ends. These ideas, which impose themselves for so many reasons, what do they lack to attain—not subjective certainty: they possess that—but the full 'objective truth' of an object of science? Kant has reiterated a hundred times: they lack being constitutive of a necessary theoretical object. While the presuppositions of sentiment are indeed 'constitutive' of our concrete action in the pursuit of specific ends, our concrete actions are never inherently and absolutely necessary in themselves. The postulates of practical reason are likewise 'constitutive' of our action, and this time, of our moral action as such, hence of an action that is absolutely necessary because purely 'obligatory': their practical value is therefore absolute. However, they do not yet enjoy that theoretical necessity that is the immediate mark of the 'true' objective. Neither the presuppositions of sentiment nor the postulates of practical reason are 'practically determinative,' as Kant explains, unless they appear as 'the only possible form of our thought,' either relative to a given action or even 'absolutely' and for any action whatsoever; they do not yet appear as 'the sole form of the possibility of objects.' Therefore, at the theoretical level, they remain 'regulative' principles of our thinking, expressions of reason's 'subjective need' for unity, nothing more.[60]

The reason for this ultimate agnosticism (as Maréchal consistently calls Kant's philosophy) is, as indicated by the final lines of the passage just quoted, the confinement of the methodological transcendentalism within a systematic transcendentalism of subjectivity. Maréchal calls Kant's draining of dynamic finality (which finality points to the objectivity of 'things in themselves') as a freezing or solidification of the "dynamic conception of the understanding"[61] into a "conception of knowledge that is too exclusively formal and static," a "sterile conceptualism."[62] However, this is nothing other than the absolutization of transcendental subjectivity.[63]

> Despite the dynamic expressions such as 'function,' 'synthetic activity,' etc., that Kant, like everyone else, uses, his demonstrations rely exclusively on fixed interconnections of a priori conditions, on a logically necessary hierarchy of 'forms' and 'rules.' In this regard, the Neo-Kantians of Marburg have hit the mark: the *Critique of Pure Reason* is primarily a nomology and methodology of reason. Kant could not completely eliminate from his mind the influence of Wolffianism: he remains in static analysis; in him, the 'transcendental' consideration, from which the conquering affirmation of the act could emerge—according to Fichte's belief—is confined to the meticulous and definitive delineation of form.[64]

Therefore, while Kant—by redirecting the transcendent

60. Maréchal, 3:235–36.
61. Maréchal, 3:238.
62. Maréchal, 5:4.
63. Maréchal, 5:426.
64. Maréchal, 3:238.

dynamic finality toward a transcendental subjectivity that reposes in itself—consolidates himself into a systematic transcendentalism of the I, in Thomas, the same dynamic finality (the 'appetitus naturalis' of knowing toward 'Being in itself' as its 'bonum') plays its 'speculative role,' as Maréchal puts it,[65] meaning it becomes the internal, theoretical foundation for the metaphysical objectivity of knowledge. It serves as the basis for a systematic transcendentalism of being, which, as such, ceases to be a 'systematic transcendentalism' in Kant's sense and becomes metaphysics.

This takes us into the second main part of Maréchal's positive thesis, into his objective-methodological[66] exposition of Thomistic epistemology as the internal overcoming and fulfillment of Kant ("Kant, the patient initiator, would be complemented rather than contradicted"[67]).

Second: the objective-methodological thesis.

If we use the title of Maréchal's book, we can formulate this thesis as follows: methodological transcendentalism (in the sense defined above)—when it is consistently carried through in keeping with its inner logic—is "le point de départ de la métaphysique" [the point of departure for metaphysics].

The proof is successful, then, when methodological transcendentalism, consistently carried through, establishes the fundamental thesis of metaphysics. However, according to Maréchal, methodological transcendentalism concludes with the dynamic finality of the transcendental act toward the 'things in themselves.' The fundamental thesis of metaphysics, as per Maréchal, is the assertion of the principle of noncontradiction in the formulation of the principle of identity ("the principle of identity or contradiction"[68]; "quod est, est" [what is, is][69]), which means an absolute

65. Maréchal, 5:6.
66. *sachmethodische.*—Trans.
67. Maréchal, 5:30.
68. Maréchal, 1:28.
69. Maréchal, 5:44, 206.

'is' (in contrast to the 'relative' nature of a pure transcendentalism that only has the 'relation' of knowledge as its foundation, i.e., it says nothing about the absolute existence-subsistence[70] of the points of the relation, both of the subject and the object, as realities). So, we have a foundation laid for the fundamental thesis of metaphysics by methodological transcendentalism when the dynamic finality not only takes the form of a 'postulate' but also, in the form of a "logical coherence,"[71] posits 'absolute Being.'

However, according to Maréchal, this occurs actually and solely in that point where dynamic finality culminates: in God as 'absolute Being.' The paradox of metaphysical knowledge—namely, that an individual and contingent subject is the bearer of the universal and the absolute ("the disturbing disproportion of an individual and contingent thought laden with universal and absolute meaning"[72])—is resolved by the dynamic-final character of knowing, as it continually moves "incessantly from the Absolute (God) to the Absolute: from the Absolute, the First Cause, which moves it with a natural motion, to the Absolute, the Final End, which it strives to reach through elicited acts."[73] Since according to Thomas, "every object of intelligence has . . . a necessary relation to the absolute of being,"[74] but on the other hand, the subjective "intellectual dynamism" is determined by the "forma generalissima entis" [most universal form of being]—i.e., has being itself as its inner meaning,[75] so, according to Maréchal, all knowledge of the objective is grounded in the "ipsum esse" of God, and therefore this "absolute Being" is "implicitly affirmed, as a 'positive noumenon' in every judgment."[76]

Maréchal's proof for this has eight steps.

70. *schlechthinnige Dasein-Bestehen.*—Trans.
71. Maréchal, 5:334.
72. Maréchal, 5:xviii.
73. Maréchal, 5:xviii.
74. Maréchal, 5:51.
75. Maréchal, 5:274ff.
76. Maréchal, 5:448.

First, it is already an ingredient of methodological transcendentalism that God is the unconditionally necessary condition for all conditions of knowledge.

Second, it is a fundamental doctrine in Thomism that the inner 'appetitus naturalis' of the intellect (its 'dynamic finality') is directed toward absolute Being, and therein toward God as 'esse ipsum': "assimilating movement tending toward an absolute final End."[77] "The subjective adequate end of our intellectual dynamism . . . consists in a saturating 'assimilation' of the form of being, in other words, in the possession of God."[78]

However, third, the possibility of this end is logically co-affirmed: "This end, although supernatural, must be, in itself, possible: otherwise, the radical tendency of our intellectual nature becomes a logical absurdity: the appetite for nothing."[79]

Then, fourth, in such an assertion of the subjective end's possibility, the possibility of the reality of God (as the objective end) is also co-affirmed:

> For the assimilation to absolute Being to be possible, it is necessary, first and foremost, that this absolute Being exists. . . . The knowing subject commits itself, by logical necessity, to this 'it is necessary.' . . . For, strictly speaking, while one can strive for a goal without certainty of reaching it, or even with the certainty that one will not, one cannot, without contradicting oneself, pursue a goal that one deems to be absolutely and, in all respects, unattainable. It would be to will nothing.[80]

Therefore, since—fifth—God, if He exists, is the 'ens necessarium,' the Necessary Being, the assertion of the possibility of His reality includes the claim of his actual, real existence.

77. Maréchal, 5:334.
78. Maréchal, 5:336.
79. Maréchal, 5:336.
80. Maréchal, 5:336.

When the 'subjective end' is a finite object, the mode of reality of the latter is not entirely determined by the mere fact of objectively 'ending' a tendency. . . . But when this object is God, when the objective end is identified with the Necessary Being in itself (Pure Act), which has no other mode of reality than absolute existence, then the dialectical demand wrapped in desire takes on a new significance—not due to the natural desire alone, but due to the object of desire: to affirm that God is possible is to affirm purely and simply that He exists, since His existence is the condition of all possibility.[81]

But now, sixth, since the subjective finality for God is an 'a priori necessity' of knowledge in general (by virtue of its 'appetitus naturalis' for 'being in itself'), ultimately, "our implicit affirmation of absolute Being" is also 'a priori necessary.'

When the subjective end is the final end, it is necessarily pursued by virtue of an a priori disposition, a natural will that is logically prior to any contingent activity. Now, to necessarily and a priori will the subjective end is to adopt its possibility necessarily and a priori; consequently, it is to necessarily and a priori affirm the (necessary) existence of the objective end. Our implicit affirmation of absolute Being bears, therefore, the mark of an a priori necessity, as was to be demonstrated.[82]

Seventh, since the objectivity of knowledge is justified in God and from God as the 'ens necessarium,' the justification of the objectivity of all knowledge takes place in proportion to the connection of the respective objects with God, i.e., based on their 'hypothetical necessity' derived from their factual origin from God. "Once the contingent representations are introduced into

81. Maréchal, 5:337.
82. Maréchal, 5:338.

the intellect's dynamism, it is a priori necessary that they relate, as subordinate ends, to the final End. Their objective existence, logically embedded in their contingent assimilation, itself relies on a necessity: *dum sunt, non possunt non esse* [while they exist, they cannot not exist]."[83]

Therefore, eighth, corresponding to this objective connection, subjective knowing essentially occurs 'in God.' "If the relationship of data to the final End of intelligence is an intrinsically constitutive a priori condition of every object of our thought, the analogical knowledge of absolute Being, as the supreme and ineffable term of this relation, 'implicitly' enters into our immediate consciousness of every object qua object."[84] And "we find this [the objective necessity of an absolute Being] implicitly affirmed as a 'positive noumenon' in every judgment,"[85] and this is "the supreme speculative guarantee demanded by critical philosophers."[86]

Certainly, thereby, the immediate vision of God (*visio beatifica*) appears in the final perspective of this critical justification of knowledge. "Indeed, our fundamental capacity extends to an ultimate end, distant but possible—our intuitive assimilation with God Himself."[87] Indeed, one can say that the arguments only pertain to the possibility of this ultimate end,[88] and that, second, by the "transcendence of infinite Being" in them, provide "the peremptory reason for our inability, both physical and juridical, to possess it directly."[89] Nonetheless, "the beatific vision of God [exists] as the ultimate object of our profound inclination," and without its bestowal, "the disproportion in man between our desire and power would be . . . glaring."[90] Thus, here, epistemology,

83. Maréchal, 5:338f.
84. Maréchal, 5:425.
85. Maréchal, 5:448.
86. Maréchal, 5:425.
87. Maréchal, 5:350.
88. Maréchal, 5:351.
89. Maréchal, 5:350.
90. Maréchal, 5:350.

like metaphysics, "opens upward." "The metaphysics of the knowing subject, if one wishes to perfect it, presents an option that
reason, left to itself, is powerless to decide."[91] By itself, "our metaphysical theory of knowledge supposes the 'non-impossibility in
itself' of an essential intuition of absolute Being."[92]

Last, Maréchal's theory certainly comes across as something
like a renewal of the theory of 'ontological intuitionism' since it
has us know everything 'in God.' However, his theory does not
involve 'seeing' but only indicates that the grounds of the objectivity of our knowledge are illuminated by reflection 'in God.'
"The affirmation of the Infinite," as the "dynamic constitutive
condition of the thought object, has nothing in common with a
'vision of objects in God,' nor with an 'innate idea,' even if only
'virtually,' in the Cartesian sense. Purely implicit and 'exercised'
in the apperception of finite objects, it can only be explicated
dialectically, through reflection and analysis."[93] This grounding
of objective knowledge in God is nothing other than "the pairing
of absolute Being and deficient participation in absolute Being,
the pairing of 'esse imparticipatum' [unparticipated being] and
'esse participatum' [participated being]," which is found at "the
bottom of our concepts (*in exercito cuiuslibet apprehensionis intel-
lectualis* [in the exercise of any intellectual apprehension])"—"the
general analogy of being."[94] It is "analogical knowledge."[95]

Despite all this, it is still true that the critical path of knowledge does not immediately proceed through sensory perception
to things[96] but solely through that "mediation" via the finality of
our knowledge toward God. This finality is "formally manifested
to the subject by the analysis of its own a priori exigencies":[97] a

91. Maréchal, 5:352.
92. Maréchal, 5:xx.
93. Maréchal, 5:453.
94. Maréchal, 1:79.
95. Maréchal, 5:350.
96. Maréchal, 5:88f.
97. Maréchal, 5:374.

path to the objectivity of things through their eternal connection with God in God,[98] a path that resides in the depths of the knowing I.[99]

While in the development of Kant through absolute idealism, "the transcendental I merges, subjectively and objectively, with the absolute principle postulated by reason at the origin of all things,"[100] here with Maréchal, from the fully-perceived transcendental I, one's gaze opens toward God and past God to things: the systematic transcendentalism of Being in sharp contrast to the transcendentalism of the I.[101]

*

The unity gained in this way is clearly that of a *critical Platonism*. Maréchal has hitherto given the only partially-expressed Platonism of Belgian-French neo-Thomism (in its formulation of a metaphysics entirely independent of the empirical sciences) its decisive epistemological justification, while simultaneously revealing its character as Platonism (and with that, the Platonism of Thomism as a school more broadly).

For Platonism—and for a 'Christian Platonism' in the sense of Augustine and Anselm—certain characteristics can be identified. First, it is characterized by the doctrine of a metaphysics of 'eternal essences,' meaning philosophy is not an exploration of the concrete individual world but an elucidation of its universal, necessary essences (*scientia universalium*). Second, it is distinguished by a consistent theory of knowledge involving an 'ascent to eternal Being' as the cognitive disposition corresponding to these 'eternal essences' (in contrast to penetration of sense perceptions). Finally, it is completed by the path to God set forth by

98. Maréchal, 5:338f.
99. Maréchal, 5:64ff., 346n2.
100. Maréchal, 5:426.
101. Maréchal, 5:40.

Anselm, i.e., from the essence of God to His existence logically entailed by it.

However, these three points are Maréchal's fundamental positions. The first corresponds to his explicitly stated presupposition of the "scientia universalium,"[102] and the second to his doctrine on the "assimilative movement" toward God's "ipsum esse" as the disposition in which knowledge objectively relates to being (the sensory element of knowledge is only the "element of representation," while the "objective signification" is determined by the "ontological relation to the Absolute"[103]), thus representing a complete renewal of the Platonic "homoiousthai theōi" [to be like God]. The third, however, is the correlative of his attaining God's existence via the insight into the idea of God as the intrinsic finality of knowledge and the possibility of God's existence as the inner condition for the actual orientation of the intellect to this end.

This explicit Platonism, however, now leads to an interpretation of Thomas (and, consequently, to a corresponding interpretation of Kant) that emphasizes 'one' side of his thought exclusively. Vis-à-vis *Thomas*, one cannot deny that the elements of Maréchal's theory are indeed found in him. It is the Platonic-Augustinian side of his thought primarily evident in the *Quaestiones disputatae de Veritate* (which Maréchal therefore prefers to cite). However, primarily by way of the commentary on Boethius's *De Trinitate* (which, with Maréchal, retreats into a dubious position) and the incisive passages on epistemology in the *Summa Theologiae*, it is equally undeniable that this side is clearly paralyzed by an Aristotelianism developed along the lines of an empirically-grounded metaphysics. Indeed, the *De Veritate* itself opposes the methodological principle forming the core of Platonism, the "reductio in

---

102. Maréchal, 1:45ff., 120ff., among others.
103. Maréchal, 5:442.

prima principia innata," with the sharp contrast of a "reductio in sensibilia."[104]

In all three points just discussed, this Aristotelianism takes the opposite standpoint to Maréchal's Thomism. In its overall concept of metaphysics, this Aristotelianism aims incipiently at a doctrine of the relationship between the universal and the individual, which lays the foundation for the later '*scientia individualium*' of Scotus and Suárez.[105] In its concept of metaphysical knowledge, it extends the causality of sensory data so strongly that even the 'first principles' appear to be traced back to them, and the strength and extent of intellectual knowledge are presented as directly dependent on the senses. Consequently, all knowledge of 'pure essences' is simply an 'effect' derived from fundamental sensory knowledge.[106] As a result, the path to God also exclusively relies on the presuppositions of the senses, to such an extent that all the content of the image [we form] of God arises from them,[107] and therefore, in this temporality, God appears as 'tamquam ignotus,' because all knowledge of the spiritual is "per negationem et remotionem."[108] This leads to the rejection of Anselm's path from Aquinas's innermost positive mindset.[109] So, Thomas's Aristotelian side stands at least on equal footing with his Platonic-Augustinian side. But the true Thomas is the relation between the two sides. Which is to say, the foundational aporetic that neo-Thomism wants to establish—but misses—is the specifically Thomistic 'in-between' of these two sides.[110]

What, then, is the deeper reason for Maréchal arriving at his

104. Thomas Aquinas, *De Veritate* 12.3 ad 2 and 3.

105. Thomas Aquinas, *Summa theologiae* 1.57.2; *Compendium theologiae* 71 and 102.

106. Thomas Aquinas, *De Trinitate* 2.6.4, 2.6.2 ad 5; *Summa theologiae* 1.85.7, 1.12.12, 1.84.7.

107. Thomas Aquinas, *Summa theologiae* 1.84.7 ad 3; 1.12.13.

108. Thomas Aquinas, *De Trinitate* 2.6.3; see also 1.2 co. and 1.2 ad 1.

109. Thomas Aquinas, *Summa theologiae* 1.2 and 1.88.3.

110. See Przywara, *Ringen der Gegenwart: Gesammelte Aufsätze, 1922–1927* (Augsburg, DE: Benno Filser, 1929), 2:906ff.

one-sided image of Thomas? We already hinted at it when we spoke of his coming to God as the justification for the objectivity of knowledge by way of the principle of identity. Indeed, this is the crux of the whole matter. Thomas does not base his entire metaphysics on the principle of identity but on the principle of noncontradiction.[111] Due to the fact that the principle of non-contradiction has a negative form ('a thing cannot both be and not be in the same respect at the same time'), it is, so to speak, internally 'in potentia' to that principle, which is the real, positive fundamental principle of his thought—namely, the principle of the 'analogia entis.'

However, if the principle of identity is taken as the basis of his thought, from its 'what is, is' only two paths are available: either the identification of this 'is' with the creature (the path of German Idealism) or its identification with God (the path of Ontologism).[112] Maréchal seeks to escape this dilemma by first discussing a synthesis of sensory knowledge and intellectual knowledge (thus excluding an intuition of pure being[113]), and second, by emphatically introducing the 'analogy' into his system.[114] But first, his 'synthesis' (according to the 'a priori objectivism') is a 'path' from the senses to pure intellect, which alone is deemed real. Second, his 'analogy,' resulting from his justification of objectivity via God, serves as an analogy 'from above to below' or an analogy of 'cognitio matutina'—that is, decidedly not a knowledge of God from and in things but knowledge of things from and in God.

To clearly distinguish Maréchal's system from Ontologism,

---

111. Thomas Aquinas, *Summa theologiae* 2-2.1.7; *Summa contra Gentiles* 2.83, etc.

112. See, in this regard, the in-depth discussions by F. M. Sladeczek on "Das Widerspruchsprinzip und der Satz von hinreichenden Grunde," in *Scholastik* 2 (1927): 1–37, at 1ff., which, however, needs to be supplemented by the relationship between the principle of noncontradiction and the principle of analogy touched on above.

113. Maréchal, *Métaphysique*, 1:145ff., etc.

114. Maréchal, 5:176ff.

one could indeed characterize it as a critical finalism of being[115]. The implied epistemology of French-Belgian neo-Thomism is otherwise the theory of an intuition of being qua being. Such a theory naturally stands in a certain proximity to Ontologism. Indeed, in light of our dilemma above, it could directly seem to affirm it (unless a distinction between God and pure being is introduced from elsewhere).

However, Maréchal is too discerning to embrace such a theory. First, he transforms the static intuition into a dynamic finality illuminated by knowledge. Second, since the *terminus a quo* is creaturely knowledge, this 'intuition in finality' also bears the character of the creaturely, somehow being an approach 'toward God from the creature and through the creature.' So, a twofold distance unfolds within the original immediacy to pure being: the distance inherent in finality qua finality and the distance emanating from the creatureliness of the *terminus a quo*.

Nevertheless, it must be acknowledged that the primary impetus of Maréchal's system is an approach 'from God to creatures,' while the elements just discussed represent his attempt to apply the brakes. If (as Maréchal sees so clearly) the scholastic summas of the Middle Ages, in terms of their epistemological stance, have a 'from God to creatures' approach (in that they philosophize from theology), then Maréchal's system is an attempt to transpose this stance from the level of 'from theology to philosophy' (where it has its unambiguously necessary meaning) to the level of 'pure philosophy,' where it unavoidably encounters significant difficulties, to say the least.

From this perspective, *Kant's* problem appears in a new light. Maréchal's only answer to why Kant does not overcome agnosticism via a priori 'objectivism' and 'dynamic finality' is to attribute it to the 'static conceptualism' he inherited from Wolff. In light

115. *kritischen Seins-Finalismus.*—Trans.

of our discussions about the principles of identity and noncontradiction, we can now delve deeper into this matter.

The fundamental reason for Kant's restrictions is, indeed, a relic of Wolff. But it is his humanist-rationalist[116] Ontologism, which derives the empirical world from 'pure being.' Since this 'pure being' shines forth in human reason as its fundamental intuition, human reason enters into a close unity with divine reason. In its fundamental intuition, human knowledge somehow possesses a divine character. Consequently, the antithesis between the human and the divine is logically transposed into the antithesis between sensory life and reason. We achieve the deification of reason in contrast to the depravity of the sensory world (or at least, in contrast to the sensory world as a dependent, undeveloped intellect[117] in Descartes and Leibniz).

As we said earlier, Kant's 'synthesis' of rationalism and empiricism is an identity of contradictions[118]. For in it, the unity of 'humanity,' which possesses divine features, presents itself as a unity in which, on the one hand, the sensory aspect appears as the 'chaotic' (up to the point of 'radical evil') in comparison to the eternal 'order' of the spiritual aspect. On the other hand, however, the spiritual aspect is so deeply intertwined with the sensory aspect that it appears as the latter's dependent formal principle and ultimately seems to be identical with it. Certainly, Kant, like Thomas, tends toward a 'synthesis' between the sensory and spiritual aspects. But through humanity's usurped divine traits in Kant, this synthesis becomes a unity of contradiction and identity. Therefore, that 'infinite progress'—in which Kant seems to signify a true renewal of the Platonic movement toward eternal being—does not present itself as a Platonism of tranquil rhythm but rather as a painful convulsion, a Platonism of tragic unrest.

Yet a genuine sense of a *'Platonic Thomas'* seems to have been

116. *humanitäts-rationalistischer.*—Trans.
117. *un-eigenständig unentwickelt Geistigen.*—Trans.
118. *Widerspruch-Identität.*—Trans.

conceded. In fact, in terms of method, we must speak of a double Platonism of Thomas Aquinas—and this is the enduring core of Maréchal's work. The first is the restless movement of knowledge arising from full life. Plato is, as the French Plato scholar [Auguste] Diès aptly puts it, "the master of those who seek,"[119] and the rich colors of sensory vividness characterize the nature of his thought. For Thomas, the words "in infinitum" ("ever further into infinity")[120] and "alia et alia conceptione" ("unto ever new conceptions")[121] stand above human knowledge. It is a knowledge whose fullness and power are bound to the fullness and power of sensory life,[122] indeed to the well-being of the body itself ("quanto corpus est melius . . ." [the better (the disposition) of a body . . .]).[123]

The second is the inner, eternal religiosity of this knowledge. In Plato, it is the solemn breath of mystery that pervades it and the 'toward God' of the 'homoiousthai theōi' at which it aims. In Thomas, it becomes that mysterious manner in which the radiance of the 'intellectus agens' is the reflection of the divine Spirit-Light[124], embodying the profound Augustinianism that forms the deep foundation of his thought. But it is the maturity of Thomas's Platonism that allows him, resting in this sacred 'in God,' to contemplate the distance between God and creature calmly and reverently. It propels the Aristotelianism of the 'causae secundae' and therein a metaphysics of the ever-changing concrete individual sensory world upward through the profound awareness of 'God all in all': "We must therefore understand that

119. Auguste Diès, *Autour de Platon: Essais de critique et d'histoire*, vol. 2, *Les Dialogues–Esquisses doctrinales* (Paris: Beauchesne, 1927), 299.

120. Thomas Aquinas, *Summa theologiae* 1.86.2 ad 4.

121. Thomas Aquinas, *De Veritate* 2.5 ad 11.

122. Thomas Aquinas, *Summa theologiae* 1.85.7.

123. Thomas Aquinas, *Summa theologiae* 1.85.7.

124. *Geist-Lichtes.*—Trans.

God works in things in such a manner that things have their proper activity."[125]

Thomas's Platonism manifests itself in his serene affirmation of the concrete world. This is neither apriorism nor aposteriorism but rather their internal unity in distinction.

II

TRANSCENDENTALISM

Kant and *transcendentalism* appear to be interchangeable concepts. Yet transcendentalism takes on a very different meaning depending on its antithesis. Transcendentalism sometimes presents itself as 'subjectivism' when juxtaposed with the 'objectivism' of Scholasticism. While, according to Thomas, it lies in the "natura" of the "ipse intellectus" "ut rebus conformetur,"[126] Kant's 'Copernican revolution' means that things (the 'mundus sensibilis') as 'matter' receive their 'form' in the categories of the subject.

Then, however, the same transcendentalism appears as 'idealism' when it is the antithesis of 'naturalism' or even 'materialism.' According to this transcendentalism, the primacy of mind over nature, of form over matter, is epistemologically grounded in the fact that things appear according to their essence only in pure *intelligere* as the act of the mind. Kant's 'shaping' and Thomas's 'abstraction' then [together] appear to be opposed to any sensualization of knowledge.

Therefore, the inner debate between Kant and Thomas does not center around the question of transcendentalism such that Kant and transcendentalism would be wholly identical. Rather, this debate appears to concern a specific understanding of transcendentalism, one that aligns precisely with what was earlier characterized as 'subjectivism.' But it also pertains, correspondingly, to emphasizing that aspect of transcendentalism that finds

---

125. Thomas Aquinas, *Summa theologiae* 1.105.5.
126. Thomas Aquinas, *De Veritate* 1.9.

expression in 'idealism.' Therefore, the debate ultimately concerns a transcendentalism that is idealism such that it is not subjectivism.

We embark on a twofold journey here. First, we aim to gain insight into Kantian transcendentalism by approaching it from the perspective of the classical problem of philosophy. Then, we carve a path out of the challenges posed by this transcendentalism, aiming to overcome Kant's philosophy from within.

*

From the pre-Socratics forward, a very general conceptual definition of philosophy emerged: it concerns the One as opposed to the many, the Necessary as opposed to the contingent, and the Eternal as opposed to the ephemeral. For the question of philosophy aims at the ultimate origin (*archē*) and ultimate goal or purpose[127] (*telos*); it aims at the first (*prōton*) and last (*eschaton*).

The things we encounter are manifold. But the relationship of diverse things to one another points back to a unity from which this diversity arises, and the progressive binding of things to each other aims toward a unity to which the diversity is directed.

The things we encounter are also contingent. For every individual thing could be other than it is and might not exist at all. Yet this entire contingent state of affairs[128]—of itself 'hanging in a void'—still manifests inner connections that point backward to a 'foundation'[129] for these contingencies (which is itself noncontingent) and forward to a 'purpose'[130] for which they strive in their inner connections (which likewise is noncontingent). This 'foundation' and 'purpose' are 'necessary,' insofar as they constitute the essential foundation and purpose for 'this' contingent state

127. *Letzten Ziel-Sinn.*—Trans.
128. *Zufälligkeit.*—Trans.
129. *Grund.*—Trans.
130. *Sinn.*—Trans.

of affairs. Thus, they are also necessary 'in themselves,' insofar as they are stable and self-standing in contrast to the contingent.

Finally, the things we encounter are ephemeral. They are in a constant state of becoming and passing away. But this continual process of becoming and passing away still 'is,' and by virtue of this 'being,' points back to a Being from which the 'being' of this process originates. A lasting influence of this Being persists through all changes: an eternity of Being within the flux of the ephemeral. Likewise, the process of becoming and passing away is subject to a hidden *telos*, which is constantly manifested within it. Thus, this telos is also something eternal within the flux, the eternally Last[131], which qua eternal is already present even now.

Origin and telos, first and last, are one and the same. The origin is only completely an origin when everything, down to the last, is from it. Thus, as origin, the telos gives direction to things. Moreover, the telos is only completely telos when everything is shaped by it. Then, it constantly stands from the beginning at the origin of things. As the telos, it is the origin. What is truly first is (as first) also last. What is truly last is (as last) also first.

So, philosophy concerns the 'Absolute.' It pertains to it in the negative sense of the word: to that which is 'isolated'—namely, isolated from the network of relationships essential for the manifold, contingent, and ephemeral. All that is 'relative'—i.e., existing in relationships—is oriented to this Absolute and, consequently, conditioned[132] by it. But the Absolute itself, as 'isolated,' lacks any relation that would ground its essence. It is, in a positive sense, the 'unconditioned,' from which and toward which everything else is conditioned. It is, as the Platonic *archē-messaton-teleutē*[133], the equally Platonic *auto kath' auto*[134], the Autonomous.

The so-called pre-Socratic 'natural philosophers' are the

131. *Ewig-Letzte.*—Trans.
132. *bedingt.*—Trans.
133. beginning, middle, and end.—Trans.
134. the thing itself.—Trans.

prototype of the *natural sciences'* response to our question: the respective 'prime element' of things is origin and telos, first and last, and thus absolute and autonomous. From it, all connections of the elements are formed and return again to its primal simplicity. Amidst the becoming and passing away of these connections, the prime element alone endures, demonstrating its independence from them while they are all conditioned by it. Hence, it is the Absolute and Autonomous.

But as the 'prime element,' it is the Absolute and Autonomous in the lowest sense, and consequently, everything above it ultimately proves illusory. Life ceases to be life, and spirit ceases to be spirit, if everything is from this lowest 'prime element' and returns to it. It is all just a masquerade of this 'prime element': masked water, fire, air, as the ancient natural philosophy proclaimed, masked helion, electron[135], as modern natural philosophy would assert. Thus, the solution of the *humanities* becomes understandable. The absolute and autonomous must be the highest of things: 'life,' 'soul,' 'spirit': the 'nous' of Anaxagoras serving as the prototype of the contemporary humanities. The innermost aspect of things is their order and their meaning. Their physical form is nothing but manifest order, realized meaning. Therefore, the primal essence—from which everything originates and toward which everything moves—is the reality that embodies such a principle of order. This is the 'immanent teleology' inherent in the essence of 'life,' which reaches its pinnacle in 'spirit.' 'Spirit' thus serves as the origin and goal, the first and last, and herein, the Absolute and Autonomous.

Only the 'prime element' and 'spirit' are realities in this creation. Are not all realities ultimately encompassed within the network of relationships of this closed world, including the 'prime element' and 'spirit'? But if the essence of the Absolute and Autonomous includes being 'isolated,' as we have explained above,

---

135. *maskiertes Helion, Elektron.*—Trans.

then how can such immanent absoluteness and autonomy still be considered genuine? Origin and goal—in the true sense of absoluteness and autonomy—can only be something that stands apart from the entire immanent reality. We thus arrive at the *Platonic solution* to the question: the 'pure ideality' of 'truth in itself,' 'goodness in itself,' and 'beauty in itself' is the sought-after Absolute and Autonomous. Truth, goodness, and beauty have their standards within themselves. They are simply the 'auto kath' auto.' Truth is 'for the sake of truth,' goodness is 'for the sake of goodness,' and beauty is 'for the sake of beauty.' However, all reality is not only measured by them but 'is' to the extent that it 'participates' in them.

Still, does this not render the mere existence[136] of reality into an 'is not' for no reason? For truth, goodness, and beauty pertain more to the 'suchness'[137] of things, to their essence[138]. Therefore, are not the realities thereby reduced to mere manifestations of the ideals of pure truth, goodness, and beauty? Isn't this tantamount to slapping reality in the face? We thus encounter the *Aristotelian solution* to the question: the ideals of truth, goodness, and beauty are indeed the Absolute and Autonomous, but not as pure, unmoved ideals above moving reality; instead, they are principles of movement within the very movement of reality itself. The Platonic ideas ('truth in itself') become the formative principles (*morphē*) of things, the Platonic values ('goodness in itself') become the 'virtues' as 'inner forces' (*energia*), and Platonic beauty becomes the harmonious 'proportion' in the universe.

Doesn't the real emphasis then logically shift to this totality? For principles of motion, however much one may wish to establish them as the 'kinoun akinēton' [unmoved mover], are ultimately 'for the purpose' of motion. With this, however, the cycle of motion, the *kuklophoria*, becomes the true Absolute and

136. *Da-Sein.*—Trans.
137. *So.*—Trans.
138. *So-Sein.*—Trans.

Autonomous. Doesn't this abolish Platonic idealism? Doesn't it represent a regression to the solutions of empirical science, albeit with the difference that this 'cycle' replaces 'prime element' and 'spirit'?

This is the issue as it stands conceptually prior to *Kantian transcendentalism*. It is the problem of Platonic idealistic transcendence, leading to a devaluation of reality, and Aristotelian idealistic immanence (in the cosmos), which tends to jeopardize ideality.

From this perspective, Kantian transcendentalism initially appears as a *synthesis* between the Platonic and Aristotelian solutions. It presupposes that the starting point of the solution, at the very least, lies in the *auto kath' auto* of truth, goodness, and beauty. Therefore, the three critiques are accordingly divided: the *Critique of Pure Reason* pertains to truth, the *Critique of Practical Reason* to goodness, and the *Critique of Judgment* to beauty. And for all three, the word applies, which is presupposed by the *Critique of Pure Reason*: they are concerned with the 'Unconditioned,' from which everything comes and toward which everything is conditioned[139]. But it is about a middle solution between Platonic transcendence and Aristotelian (cosmic) immanence. Kant is seeking a realm of truth, goodness, and beauty that, on the one hand, surpasses the real world but, on the other, is not so superior that it is entirely separate from it. It must therefore be one that points to a 'beyond,' a 'trans,' but in such a way that it is not a realm definitively above and beyond[140], a 'transcendent realm,' but one that, while standing in the real world, 'pertains to the beyond (the 'trans'),' i.e., is '*trans*cendental.'

This general idea of transcendentalism is realized in the 'mind'[141] as it exists in the 'human.' The pure ideality of truth, goodness, and beauty springs forth in the acts of the mind: truth

139. *zu dem alles hin bedingt sei.*—Trans.
140. *Über-hinaus-gestiegenes.*—Trans.
141. *Geist.*—Trans.

in thinking, goodness in willing, beauty in feeling. Truth-in-itself, goodness-in-itself, and beauty-in-itself are simply manifestations of that inner, dynamically active absoluteness found in thinking-in-itself, willing-in-itself, and feeling-in-itself, respectively. This denotes the autonomous spontaneity or spontaneous autonomy that ascends from thinking to willing, culminating in its 'pure expression' in the 'sheer purposelessness' of the aesthetic. This transcendentalism, as the *active transcendentalism of the mind*, concerns, on the one hand, the pure ideality of truth, goodness, and beauty. It is not about 'dynamically active absoluteness' in the sense of the natural intensity or quality of the empirical acts of thinking, willing, or feeling. Nor is it concerned with a real entity 'in act.' Rather, Kantian transcendentalism is about the pure ideality (of truth, goodness, and beauty) 'in act.' Truth, goodness, and beauty are themselves 'transcendental,' i.e., their dynamically active absoluteness in thinking-in-itself, willing-in-itself, and feeling-in-itself, 'pertains to' the 'trans' of their pure idea-form.

But on the other hand, this dynamically active absoluteness takes place 'in the human' and so 'within the limits' of the human, although not within the limits of person X as opposed to the limits of person Y, but within the limits of human nature in general, i.e., 'within the limits of humanity.' The human, however, qua human, is directed toward the sensory-natural universe. Therefore, if the active transcendentalism of the mind occurs in humans, then still it occurs—inasmuch as it pertains to the pure ideality of truth, goodness, and beauty—with an eye to the natural world.

Thus, Kantian transcendentalism seems to resolve in one fell swoop the entire problem of philosophy as a whole. The truth of the solution of the natural sciences is preserved: that the first and last must truly stand 'within' nature. Yet this truth is preserved such that the primacy of the mind, as rightly emphasized by the solution of the humanities, remains untouched and is even underscored. For the mind is directed toward nature that it may shape nature. On the other hand, the mind is not taken as an empirical reality but as 'ideality in act' and so corresponds to the solution of Platonic idealism. However, considering that it is still the 'mind' in which this 'ideality in act' occurs and, as ideality *in act*, unfolds dynamically, the important thing in Aristotle's response is safeguarded: inclusion within the dynamism of the universe.

*

Kantian transcendentalism as a synthesis depends on the interplay of two determinations. This interplay becomes its fate and its internal critique.

The first interplay in it concerns the *relationship between ideality and reality*. On the one hand, the sensory reality of the world is merely 'matter' for 'ideality in act.' On the other hand, this 'ideality in act' is inherently directed toward the sensory reality of the world. This is a forced unity that inevitably had to fracture, and when it fractured, it fractured into the contradiction between Hegel's absolute idealism and the absolute materialism of Feuerbach and Marx.

For *Hegel*'s absolute idealism, the sensory reality of the world is nothing more than the manifestation of 'ideality in act,' and this 'ideality in act' itself has become 'idea in act,' no longer (as with Kant) the inner absolute of thinking, willing, and feeling, but rather the inner dynamism of the idea itself. For *Feuerbach*'s and *Marx*'s absolute materialism, however, the (Kantian) inner reference of 'ideality in act' to the sensory reality of the world has, on the contrary, become independent, until this 'ideality in act' has been reduced to being merely a manifestation of this sensory reality. The 'in act' has remained for both absolute idealism and absolute materialism and within them has evolved into 'dialectic':

in Hegel, into the straightforward 'dialectic of the idea,' in Feuer-bach and Marx, into the 'dialectic of matter.'

This already touches on the fate of the second interplay in Kantian transcendentalism. Insofar as it represents a transcen-dentalism of the human mind, the 'synthetic unity of the I' be-comes central to it: within the unity of the I, thinking-in-itself, willing-in-itself, and feeling-in-itself are bound together. But with this, the antithesis between ideality and reality enters into this very I. It is, on the one hand, *ideality as the I* (the 'transcen-dental subject'). But this 'ideality as the I' is nevertheless nowhere else but in the 'real I' (the 'empirical subject'). The 'synthesis' is essentially an 'ideative synthesis'—namely, the synthesis of the threefold 'ideality in act' (thinking-in-itself, willing-in-itself, feeling-in-itself). Yet it is solely realized within the empirically real synthesis of the empirically real subject. This is the innermost forced unity of the forced unity discussed above, which is why it breaks apart even more forcefully.

Hegel's absolute idealism is based on such a synthetic ideation that every I-character[142] is extinguished, and instead of a unity of the I, the unity of the 'it' of the idea takes precedence. The abso-lute materialism of Feuerbach and Marx, on the other hand, has as its internal complement the absoluteness of the real-empirical I: *Stirner*'s 'unique individual' and *Nietzsche*'s 'Übermensch.' In both of these mutually contradictory directions, there remains a final common formal aspect, wherein both adhere to Kantian transcendentalism: the 'synthesis in act.' But in Hegel, it is the innermost principle of the 'dialectic of the idea': the enduring I of the idea as it undergoes the stages of thesis, antithesis, and synthe-sis. In Stirner and Nietzsche, it is the innermost principle of the 'dialectic of matter': the revolutionary pathos, breaking through all barriers, of the robust, biological I.

From this fate, however, arises the internal critique of

---

142. *I-Charakter.*—Trans.

transcendentalism. It unfolds first in the progression from neo-Kantianism to phenomenology. But it then unfolds more deeply in the philosophy of religion's critique of foundations.

The progression from *neo-Kantianism* to *phenomenology* engages with the interplay between ideality and reality, which became the fate of Kantian transcendentalism. This fate was sealed by the concept of a purely dynamic ideality. After all, to think, will, and feel is 'to think, will, and feel something.' And if this 'something' is only sensory reality, then it is no wonder that from an 'ideality in act,' ultimately nothing emerges but an internal 'in act' of this sensory reality, the mind as a revolutionary force shaping matter. It is therefore important to enhance this 'ideality in act' with a 'something' that internally determines its dynamism. Marburg *neo-Kantianism* (Cohen and Natorp[143]) does this through its 'ideas as methods,' and Baden neo-Kantianism (Windelband and Rickert[144]) does this through its 'values as standards,' indeed, 'values as true being.' Thinking-in-itself, willing-in-itself, feeling-in-itself is an 'infinite progress' that strives toward the 'being' of pure ideas or values and is thus internally directed by them. But in neo-Kantianism, these ideas or values are ultimately only 'methods,' i.e., internal orientations of 'ideality in act.' The completion of the idea underlying neo-Kantianism is therefore only achieved when the 'something' (in 'thinking, willing, and feeling something') internally constitutes this thinking, willing, and feeling itself. This, however, is the fundamental concept of *phenomenology*: the essential 'intentionality of consciousness.' Consciousness as thinking, willing, and feeling (as 'noesis') is internally determined by the 'something' of this thinking, willing, and feeling (by the 'noema'). This completes the struggle against naturalism. For it now belongs to the inner essence of 'ideality in act' that, as 'noesis' (thinking, willing, feeling), it is internally

143. Hermann Cohen and Paul Natorp.—Trans.
144. Wilhelm Windelband and Heinrich Rickert.—Trans.

determined by the noematic of truth-in-itself, goodness-in-itself, beauty-in-itself.

But what about the positive aspect of the relationship of this noesis-noema ideality to reality? For surely Kant's forced unity is not redeemed by merely removing ideality's dangerous ties to reality. This critique of Kantian transcendentalism unfolds in the development of phenomenology from *Husserl* to Scheler to *Heidegger*.

In the universal transcendentalism of truth, goodness, and beauty, the 'something' (something as true, something as good, something as beautiful) obviously does not mean simply what Husserl thinks it does: the noematic-ideative something of 'pure essences.' Rather, this 'something' essentially refers to some existing thing[145]. Something 'is' true, something 'is' good, something 'is' beautiful. Truth, goodness, and beauty are transcendentals—i.e., they relate to the transcendent insofar as they relate to being as transcendent. Truth, goodness, and beauty are, therefore, in the fullest sense, ultimately being's self-disclosure. They disclose its theoretical sense (the 'true'), its dynamic tendency (the 'good'), and how it oscillates within itself anticipating its perfection (the 'beautiful'). The old antithesis between natural science and the humanities, empirical science and ideal science (a tension that was only balanced in Kantian transcendentalism), is actually eliminated here. For everything is reduced to the issue of being [*Sein*] between essence and existence [*Sosein und Dasein*]. The 'true' is found in the 'essence of existence' [*So des Da*], the 'good' is found in the 'orientation of essence to existence' [*So zum Da*] or in the 'orientation of existence to essence' [*Da zum So*] (i.e., in the actualization of essence [*So-Wirklichung*] or form of existence [*Da-Gestalt*]), and the 'beautiful' is found in 'essence in existence' [*So im Da*] and 'existence in essence' [*Da im So*]. This transcendentalism of being, however, apparently has its

145. *ein Seiendes.*—Trans.

center—corresponding to Kantian transcendentalism—in a similar expression of the synthesis of the I[146] toward being. For Kant, the universal 'ideality in act' (of truth, goodness, and beauty as thinking, willing, and feeling) is concentrated in the 'synthetic unity of the I.' Heidegger is therefore methodologically correct when he traces this 'synthetic unity of the I' back to being, i.e., when he wants his teaching on truth, goodness, and beauty as the self-disclosure of being to have its center in his teaching on the 'synthetic unity of the I' as the self-disclosure of the being of the I.

But at the same time, this is the critical point. Heidegger himself in this way reaches a new form of Kant's forced unity. The being of the I, whose self-disclosure is the 'synthetic unity of the I,' is intrinsically being-in-the-world[147]. For it is the unity of that being whose self-disclosure is truth, goodness, and beauty. But this is precisely why, conversely, being-an-I is being-in-the-world. For that being, whose self-disclosure is truth, goodness, and beauty, unfolds within[148] this being-an-I. The I is the world, and the world is the I. But this is a heightened version of what is found in Kant: ideality (within the I), which is directed to reality (the world), and reality (the world), which as matter aims at ideality (within the I).

Yet beneath the surface—contrary to Heidegger's intention—something else is going on. If truth, goodness, and beauty are to be traced back to being, for him it is being as it immediately presents itself, and more so presents itself in the being of the I: not an ideal being at rest but being in becoming, in its tension between essence and existence. Heidegger, then, seeks to preserve the Absolute inherent in truth, goodness, and beauty by transforming it into a new, dynamic Absolute: into the inner, absolute dynamism of this being in becoming, which unfolds itself

146. *Ich-Synthese.*—Trans.
147. *Welt-Sein.* Shorthand for Heidegger's *in-der-Welt-sein.*—Trans.
148. *zusammenschließt sich.*—Trans.

restlessly as an 'in-the-world'[149]. But this is evidently more of a grasping for a solution than a grasping of one[150]. For Heidegger must himself logically concede that this being in becoming, if one takes seriously its self-contained nature, stands in the Nothing as the ground of its being. But then his reduction of truth, goodness, and beauty to being is ultimately a reduction to the Nothing, i.e., in plain contradiction to what is said of truth, goodness, and beauty. For they clearly bear witness to an 'is' and one that really is a pure 'Is': *Veritas Ipsa, Bonitas Ipsa, Pulchritudo Ipsa.*[151]

Thus, we find ourselves in the second critique, which historically unfolds in relation to Kantian transcendentalism: the critique of the *philosophy of religion.* For the Platonism of the transcendent-static truth, goodness, and beauty—as well as for the Aristotelianism of the immanent-dynamic truth, goodness, and beauty—the divine was still a kind of background. But the tendency of Platonism nevertheless aimed at replacing the world of the gods with the divinity of truth, goodness, and beauty, and in Aristotelianism, the divinity of this truth, goodness, and beauty (as *noēsis noēseōs* [thought thinking itself] and *kinoun akinēton* [unmoved mover]) slides so readily into the *kuklophoria* [cycle of motion] of the universe that, actually, this universe is the divine. This logically extends to Kantian transcendentalism as well, which mediates between Platonism and Aristotelianism. The center of this mediation, as we have seen, is the 'synthetic unity of the I' in the human. Consequently, the divine must allow itself to be tailored to fit human standards. This leads to Kant's "religion within the bounds of mere reason," i.e., religion measured by the meaning and utility of humanity. God is oriented toward humanity, and therefore it logically follows that God is not the seat of absolute truth, goodness, and beauty as their sole

149. *als das eine 'In der Welt' sich restlos zusammenschließt.*—Trans.
150. *eine Lösung im Zu-griff als im Be-griff.*—Trans.
151. Truth Itself, Goodness Itself, Beauty Itself.—Trans.

standard and judge, but the 'spirit' in 'humanity' is. It is 'Deus in nobis': humanity as the true divine.

The decisive critique occurs today at this juncture. From *Heidegger*'s perspective, the 'destruction' (to use his term) of Kant's 'ideal man' is realized in the real human of 'Care'[152] in 'the Nothing' toward 'death.' Certainly, Heidegger intends this disillusionment as the foundation for a 'pessimism of strength' in the manner of Nietzsche. But this is a stretch[153]. What remains as an insight is that humans are intrinsically in becoming[154]: their "est non est," "being and yet not being," as Augustine says.

From the pole opposite Heidegger, from *Karl Barth*'s standpoint, the relationship between God and humanity is reversed. God is no longer measured against an ideal humanity; instead, humanity is regarded as nothing before the majesty of God's Is, utterly at his disposal. According to Barth, we no longer have a humanist 'pure spirit,' in which all 'mythology' of revelation is 'cleared up'; rather, all creation is regarded as chaos under the becoming of the 'Holy Spirit.'

It is clear what happens to truth, goodness, and beauty in this view. It is the same thing that happened, quite decisively, in *Augustine*'s and *Thomas Aquinas*'s philosophy: God as Truth, Goodness, and Beauty. What arose from this confrontation between Heidegger and Karl Barth is the idea of man as nothing before God's Is. If this idea is true, then the Absolute and Autonomous, which truly lies in truth, goodness, and beauty, is not the self-disclosure of human being or of that of any creature at all. It is the self-disclosure of the Being of God, who alone is Absolute and Autonomous. Truth, Goodness, and Beauty mean *Deus Ipsa Veritas*, *Deus Ipsa Bonitas*, and *Deus Ipsa Pulchritudo*. They are the luminous, innermost self-revelation of God. Following the profound hints Augustine hazards in *De Trinitate*, we can say that

152. *Sorge.*—Trans.
153. *Zu-griff.*—Trans.
154. *innere Werdehaftigkeit.*—Trans.

they are a luminosity in which God's innermost life sketches its mystery in 'traces': the Trinity. But then the foundational nature of God's autonomy is logically expressed in the formula for the autonomy of truth, goodness, and beauty. The *auto kath' auto*, 'truth for the sake of truth,' 'goodness for the sake of goodness,' and 'beauty for the sake of beauty' are valid, therefore, insofar as: 'truth for the sake of God-Truth,' 'goodness for the sake of God-Goodness,' 'beauty for the sake of God-Beauty.'

However, this ultimately leads to what we can call *the subjective pathos and ethos of truth, goodness, and beauty*: humanity's subjective formal attitude in the realm of truth, goodness, and beauty. In Kantian transcendentalism, everything is objectively concentrated in the 'synthetic unity of the I.' This is subjectively expressed, with an inherent inevitability, in a dual emphasis on the I. First, there is an emphasis on the I insofar as the absolute accent slides onto it. This results in rigidity, for an absolute I surely demands majesty. So, Georg Simmel speaks of Kantian knowledge's intolerance with respect to truth. So, Schiller speaks of the Kantian fanaticism of duty with respect to the good. So, Goethe speaks, regarding the beautiful (which tolerates such rigidity the least), of "the Graces fleeing" before Kant. The corollary to this rigidity is, on the other hand, Kantian pessimism. For such an ossification of the 'absolute posture' is inherently unsustainable. As a result, it is constantly on the verge of explosion, and in the event of an explosion, of exploding into an absolute, despairing chaos. So, the pole opposite absolute rigidity is the constant awareness of 'radical evil': demonism within majesty.

It is clear how fundamentally this subjective pathos and ethos changes in the transcendentalism of Augustine and Thomas Aquinas. God is *Veritas*, *Bonitas*, and *Pulchritudo Ipsa*, and consequently, humanity is in possession of truth, goodness, and beauty insofar as it "lives, moves, and has its being" in God. Truth, goodness, and beauty do not depend on the human being; instead, the human stands in their radiance and serves them, to the extent that he stands in the radiance of the divine Majesty and is in Its service. Consequently, the serenity[155] of the serving child permeates all his pursuit of the truth, all his striving for good. Thus, the very essence of beauty in this person is precisely the form of 'liberated oscillation'[156]. Living from and in the grace of *Deus-Veritas*, *Deus-Bonitas*, and *Deus-Pulchritudo*, man is shaped in the most delicate way by this grace[157]: the 'gracefulness'[158] of the *gratia Dei*. His life becomes a graceful one[159] of constant intimacy in worship and adoring intimacy. A life like this is untouched by the pessimism of 'radical evil.' It has the audacity of Augustine's prayer, forgetting itself and the world in God: "Deus per quem universitas etiam cum sinistra parte perfecta est," "God, through whom the universe—even with its incongruous part—is perfect."[160] This kind of transcendentalism is one in which the 'trans' of truth, goodness, and beauty—which flashes forth in thinking, willing, and feeling—touches upon the most essential *Trans*: that of *Deus incomprehensibilis*, the far side of whose incomprehensibility is, however, the incomprehensibility of love. This is the true transcendentalism that all other [transcendentalisms] still intend, even when they err. For Augustine prays an even bolder prayer: "Deus in quo sunt omnia, cui tamen nec turpitudo turpis est, nec malitia nocet, nec error errat," "God in Whom all things exist, but to Whom ugliness is not ugly, malice does not harm, and error is not error."[161] Truth, goodness, and

155. *Gelöstheit.*—Trans.

156. *befreite Schwingen.*—Trans.

157. *Gnade.*—Trans.

158. *Grazie.* While *Gnade* is the usual German word for theological grace, the word used here, *Grazie*, has connotations of good social etiquette, a graceful manner.—Trans.

159. *Grazie.*—Trans.

160. Augustine, *Soliloquies* 1.1.2; I have translated Przywara's own German translation of Augustine's Latin, which reads: "Gott, durch den das All auch mit seinem Links vollkommen ist."—Trans.

161. Augustine, 1.1.2; As above, I have translated directly from Przywara's own German translation, which reads: "Gott, in Dem alles ist, dem aber Häßlichkeit nicht häßlich ist, Bosheit nicht schadet, Irrtum nicht Irrtum ist."—Trans.

beauty are so triumphantly rooted in this Trans of the incomprehensible God of love that their very opposite (*error, malitia, turpitudo*) fades away in its presence. This is transcendentalism as the most triumphant idealism because and to the extent that it is the most radical overcoming of subjectivism: the words of the Gospel turned into a system: "he who loses his life, saves it."

III

METAPHYSICS

There was a time when, in Kant's name, all metaphysics was considered finished: whether for the sake of a Kant of 'pure natural sciences' or a Kant of 'pure epistemology.' Furthermore, there was a time when it was believed that he had only eliminated an intellectual-theoretical metaphysics but had paved the way for a voluntaristic one. Heinz Heimsoeth then attempted (in his studies for Kant's jubilee) to develop this last interpretation in such a way that it would transition from a voluntaristic metaphysics to a metaphysics of personal spontaneity, which already finds its starting point in intellectual spontaneity (in the *Critique of Pure Reason*). From Riehl and Messer,[162] finally, date the not always very successful attempts to connect Kantian criticism with a critical, inductive metaphysics.

It is only in the antithesis of two new interpretations of Kant—Martin Heidegger's (*Kant und das Problem der Metaphysik*[163]) and Eugen Herrigel's (*Die metaphysische Form*[164])—that the question of Kant and metaphysics emerges in its proper form. This form is concerned with the immanent metaphysics of Kant's fundamental question, "How are synthetic a priori judgments

---

162. Alois Riehl and Wilhelm August Messer.—Trans.

163. Martin Heidegger, *Kant und das Problem der Metaphysik* (Bonn, DE: Friedrich Cohen, 1929). [English citations of this work are taken from: Martin Heidegger, *Kant and the Problem of Metaphysics*, trans. Richard Taft , 5th ed. (Bloomington, IN: Indiana University Press, 1997).—Trans.]

164. Eugen Herrigel, *Die metaphysische Form: eine Auseinandersetzung mit Kant*, vol. 1, *Der mundus sensibilis* (Tübingen, DE: Mohr, 1929).

possible?" The old antitheses—between a sensualistic Kantian-
ism, which interprets Kant's fundamental question within the
confines of sensory experience, and an idealistic Kantianism,
which interprets the same question within the apriorism of ideal
forms—now receive their deepest foundation: in the antithesis
between a fundamental metaphysics of finitude (in Heidegger)
and an equally fundamental metaphysics of infinity (in Herrigel).
However, objectively and philosophically[165], this is where Kant
and Thomas confront each other face to face: in Kant, the aporia
between a metaphysics of finitude and a metaphysics of infinity,
and in Thomas, in response, the metaphysics of the *analogia entis*.

The method of our investigation is thus given to us. We
must lead the problem of a metaphysics of finitude or infinity
from Kant beyond Heidegger and Herrigel to the point where
the question of a metaphysics of the *analogia entis* immediately
arises. We must develop the decisive approach to the metaphysics of the *analogia entis* from the problem of the metaphysics of
finitude or infinity.

*

As Heidegger and Herrigel rightly see, Kant confronts traditional
metaphysics with his fundamental line of inquiry. His line of inquiry confronts it such that his entire approach is born from it.
For the 'a priori' (of 'a priori synthetic judgments') concerns a
framework that is 'prior' to and underlies all empirical, scientific
aspects [of thinking], first and foremost. That is, it concerns the
genuine autonomy of metaphysics in relation to the empirical
sciences. However, the term 'synthetic' indicates that this framework should be examined in its internal coherence with the one,
existing world of experience. That is, it concerns metaphysics as
an internal metaphysics of the empirical sciences. Kant's line of
inquiry first aims (in the reduction to the question of judgment)

165. *sach-philosophisch.*—Trans.

at a *critical metaphysics*, i.e., at a metaphysics that does not simply approach objects naïvely but first examines its methodological possibilities and limits. Second, however, it aims at such a critical metaphysics in a double sense. In 'metaphysics in relation to the empirical sciences,' the tendency is toward a critical metaphysics of a priori forms that precedes the finite existentiality of this world: a critical metaphysics of infinity. However, in 'metaphysics as internal metaphysics of the empirical sciences,' the tendency is toward a critical metaphysics of this existing finite world: a critical metaphysics of finitude.

Both tendencies are present in Kant. For his position regarding traditional metaphysics is ambiguous. On the one hand, it is directed against a 'fanciful' metaphysics that does not heed the limits of human sensory experience. This tendency emphasizes, against Leibniz and Wolff, the metaphysical skepticism of the natural sciences. It demands sober confinement within the limits of finitude. It does so through a critical delineation of boundaries in the realm of objects: the finite human being is denied any vision beyond sensory finitude. It does so even more incisively through a critical delineation of boundaries in the act of knowing itself: according to its very nature, human knowledge is only capable of grasping sensory finitude. It rounds this off by reinterpreting everything that is non-sensory-finite[166]: the soul, the universe, God as pure limit ideas of the inner, finite 'infinite *progressus.*' In this *critical metaphysics of finitude*, infinity finally becomes the inner infinity of finitude: its formal 'infinite intensity.' As a result, the 'est Deus in nobis' of the *Opus posthumum* is accented as 'est Deus in *nobis.*' It is the divinity of humanity insofar as what is in the world coalesces around it: the earthly divinity of finite humans in the world, [reaching out] into the world[167]. It

166. *Nicht-sinnenhaft-endlichen.*—Trans.
167. *in der Welt in die Welt hinein.*—Trans.

places such an emphasis on the 'nobis' that 'nobis' appears (from below) as 'Deus': the pantheistic 'Divine Humanity.'

On the other hand, just as it is critically directed against Leibniz and Wolff, Kant's critical metaphysics is undeniably also directed against a subordination of freedom, person, and mind under the purely natural [categories] of law and extension, as is the danger with Spinozism. Kant's transcendentalism (precisely in the progression from the *Critique of Pure Reason* to the *Critique of Practical Reason*) aims at a critically secured form of a metaphysics of the primacy of freedom, person, and mind. It aims at a critical primacy of the infinity of the *mundus intelligibilis*. From this perspective, the critical delineation of boundaries in the realm of objects takes on the meaning of a positive critique. It critically safeguards the intelligible supra-finite[168] in contrast to pure nature. Likewise, the critical delineation of boundaries in the act of knowing takes on a positive aspect. It is not only a rejection of the competence of mathematical and experimental knowledge for the purely metaphysical; it also discloses a path into this metaphysical within the categories of this natural knowledge itself. This final tendency thus leads to the inverse of what we just saw: sensory finitude is only matter in relation to an infinite world of forms. The 'infinite *progressus*' speaks rather of the negative boundlessness of a capacity for reception in this matter and the positive infinity of the forms that manifest within it. The 'transcendental I' is construed from the top down: as a demiurge in service of infinity. In this *critical metaphysics of infinity*, finitude thus becomes, as it were, the 'lowest hem' of the unfolding infinity, its 'here and now' within finitude. The 'est Deus in nobis' accentuates itself as 'est *Deus in* nobis.' It is the divinity of humanity insofar as humanity manifests the supra-mundane: heavenly divinity in finite humans, not of the world, though in the world. Such is the

---

168. *Über-Endlichen.*—Trans.

emphasis on the 'Deus in' that 'Deus' (from above) appears as 'nobis': the theopanistic 'Divine Humanity.'

These internal antitheses of a critical metaphysics—found in Kant himself but without being brought to light by him—have become a conscious either/or in the antithesis of Heidegger's and Herrigel's interpretations of Kant. Our problem has thus been explicitly stated. Consequently, we will best be able to view it in the explicit form of the initial question: the problem of the formal act of metaphysics, [and with it] the problem of its formal object.

For *Heidegger*, the *metaphysics of finitude* (of 'human beings' 'in the world') is crucially grounded in the fact that [1] not only is "the mode of understanding the act of understanding itself" the "dependency upon intuition"[169] but also that [2] the understanding itself arises from the transcendental faculty of imagination, which, however, leads back to what constitutes finitude as such: time. The apriorism of the understanding is therefore an apriorism of the imagination, "a pre-forming . . . which represents 'from out of itself,'"[170] a "conceiving [*Sichdenkens*]" or "pure imagining."[171] Thus, it aligns with schematism. This is Kant's original conception, which still dominates the first edition of the *Critique of Pure Reason*. The second edition flees from the radicalism of this idea.[172]

Metaphysics is here a metaphysics of finitude because its *formal act* is itself constituted by the essence of finitude: sensory spatial-temporality[173]. Metaphysical thinking fundamentally means a thinking in which this sensory spatial-temporality appears in its 'pure form.' But this is the transcendental imagination. And so, on the one hand, it is strictly finite thinking: not only the unity of "a finite, purely sensible reason,"[174] but one that,

169. Heidegger, *Kant*, 140. [Heidegger, *Kant and the Problem of Metaphysics*, 104.]

170. Heidegger, 143. [Heidegger, *Kant and the Problem of Metaphysics*, 106.]

171. Heidegger, 144. [Heidegger, *Kant and the Problem of Metaphysics*, 106.]

172. Heidegger, 159ff.

173. *sinnenhafte Raum-Zeit-lichkeit.*—Trans.

174. Heidegger, 188. [Heidegger, *Kant and the Problem of Metaphysics*, 137.]

in its fundamental act, the "understanding of Being," is the "most finitude in what is finite"[175] because this fundamental act is rooted in "holding-itself-into-the-Nothing."[176] But on the other hand, it is a finite thinking that reinterprets infinite thinking, i.e., the absolute thinking of idealism, within its finitude, for the sake of the (active[177]) coherence of finitude. It carries within itself the power of the spontaneity of this infinite thinking: as the power of "Care" for the "potentiality-to-be-finite,"[178] for the determined "perishing [*Verendlichung*]."[179] It also carries within itself the freedom of the a priori nature of this infinite thinking: as the freedom of the transcendental imagination (upon which every other freedom is founded), forming therein "the look of the horizon of objectivity as such . . . before the experience of the being."[180] Finally, it carries within itself the transcendence of this infinite thinking: the transcendence of the a priori nature of the transcendental imagination over the 'experience of being' and the transcendence of the 'experience of being' over this 'horizon of objectivity' in general. Thus, it embodies both the first idealistic and the second realistic transcendence as a single mutual transcendence between man and the world in the immanence of finitude.

It is evident that with this, the *formal object* of metaphysics is unequivocally determined. The perceptible sensory world in its sensory nature[181] corresponds to the transcendental imagination. That is, the formal object of the metaphysics of finitude is not an 'intelligible structure' of this sensory world but rather its vital 'mood': boredom, anxiety, care, etc., which come to sheer appearance in the transcendental imagination. By further grounding the transcendental imagination in 'time,' not only does the

175. Heidegger, 219. [Heidegger, *Kant and the Problem of Metaphysics*, 160.]
176. Heidegger, 228. [Heidegger, *Kant and the Problem of Metaphysics*, 167.]
177. *akthaften.*—Trans.
178. Heidegger, 207. [Heidegger, *Kant and the Problem of Metaphysics*, 152.]
179. Heidegger, 207. [Heidegger, *Kant and the Problem of Metaphysics*, 152.]
180. Heidegger, 124. [Heidegger, *Kant and the Problem of Metaphysics*, 92.]
181. *die anschauliche Sinnenwelt in ihrer Sinnenhaftigkeit.*—Trans.

closed temporality 'correspond' to it in the sphere of objects, but act and object are one in this 'time.' Therefore, it is completed in this 'Nothing.' The fundamental act of 'finite thinking' is 'holding-itself-into-the-Nothing,' and the inner essence of closed finitude is this same 'Nothing.' "Understanding Being" means "holding-itself-into-the-Nothing,"[182] "Da-sein means: being held out into the nothing."[183] But just as finitude carries infinity within itself: standing within the Nothing, from the Nothing it encompasses "beings as a whole": "Being held out into the nothing—as Dasein is—on the ground of concealed anxiety is its surpassing of beings as a whole. It is transcendence."[184]

For *Herrigel*, conversely, a *metaphysics of infinity* (the "original syntheses" that arise from a "pure knowledge"[185]) is grounded in the Kantian 'pure understanding' being so 'pure' that it is not 'our' understanding but the "form . . . of that pure knowledge which creates worlds in original syntheses."[186] The apriorism of understanding does not point downward, into the transcendental imagination and from there into time, but rather upward into a 'pure knowledge,' to which 'our' knowledge must 'conform': into a "pure understanding" that is simultaneously a "spontaneous unity in which the pure concepts are objectively[187] founded," and an "objective unity of the original assertions[188], which are objectively established by these pure concepts":[189] an "utterly supra-logical being," from which "the real existence of sensory nature and our knowledge of its existence" derives.[190] This is Kant's conception,

182. Heidegger, 228. [Heidegger, *Kant and the Problem of Metaphysics*, 167.]

183. Martin Heidegger, *Was ist Metaphysik?* (Bonn, DE: Friedrich Cohen, 1929), 20. [English citations of this work are taken from: Martin Heidegger, "What is Metaphysics?" in *Basic Writings*, ed. David Farrell Krell (London: Harper, 2008), 89–110 at 103.—Trans.]

184. Heidegger, *Was ist Metaphysik?*, 24. [Heidegger, *What is Metaphysics?*, 106.]

185. Herrigel, *Die metaphysische Form*, 37.

186. Herrigel, 37.

187. *sachlich.*—Trans.

188. *Setzungen.*—Trans.

189. Herrigel, 38.

190. Herrigel, 183.

aligning with the progression from the first to the second edition of the *Critique of Pure Reason*. However, even in the second edition, this advance is not consistently realized.[191]

Metaphysics here is thus a metaphysics of infinity since its *formal act* already stems from original (personal) infinity: pure understanding as the 'within us' of the original understanding, which "creates worlds in original syntheses."[192] Metaphysical thinking fundamentally denotes a mode of thought in which true infinity manifests itself: in the a priori spontaneity and spontaneous a priori nature of pure understanding, as "the utterly pure will as the ground of all grounds, and together with it, the personal spiritual essence as the source of all being."[193] The fundamental act of this metaphysical thinking is, therefore, the utmost state of being "conformed" to the Is of this "supra-logical being." For the "Copernican standpoint" rests upon the absoluteness of this "supra-logical" understanding within the "absolutely pure will" of the "personal spiritual essence as the source of all being."[194] In this state of being 'conformed,' the finitude of our knowledge is thus preserved. Indeed, this preservation occurs not only through the 'adaequatio' of this being 'conformed,' which corresponds to the finite's relation to the infinite. It is also heightened by the fact that this conformity presents itself as a "demand" to us, a demand "not made by us to ourselves," but "imposed on us whether we want it or not,"[195] and as a demand "toward the infinite."[196]

This naturally also determines the *formal object* of metaphysics. 'Our' pure understanding as the 'within us' of the original understanding corresponds to the view of the 'original syntheses' in their correlation to 'matter in general.' This correlation, however,

191. Herrigel, 128f., 149ff.
192. Herrigel, 37.
193. Herrigel, 185.
194. Herrigel, 36ff.
195. Herrigel, 173.
196. Herrigel, 175.

if we were to transfer it into the language of Thomas Aquinas, is a fabric of three infinities: the *infinitum actuale* of 'pure form,' the *infinitum potentiale* of 'pure matter,' and, consequently, (what we might call) an *infinitum relationale* of the correlation between the two. Certainly, 'our' understanding is directed toward the perceptible sensory world, but first (in the "laws of nature") toward the "pure existence of a sensory nature in general";[197] second, toward the *mundus sensibilis* not for its own sake, but for the sake of "the non-given intelligible being";[198] and third, as a pathway toward understanding the pure structure between "form in itself" and "matter in itself."[199] So here, too, everything aims toward a final unity. The fundamental act of the metaphysics of infinity is the 'demanded' being-'conformed'[200] of 'our' knowledge to the "pure knowledge that creates worlds in original syntheses." The same "pure knowledge" is thus, as the "source of all being,"[201] the source of that objective essence of infinity (as we have seen): *infinitum relationale* between *infinitum actuale* and *infinitum potentiale*. Therefore, by abiding within infinite knowledge, the fundamental act of metaphysics resides in infinite being. But in contemplating this infinite being from the vantage point of the finitude of the *mundus sensibilis*, and in so doing, delving deeper into the *mundus sensibilis* from the standpoint of infinite being,[202] the object of this metaphysics of infinity remains finitude, yet finitude fundamentally in its derivation from infinity, as its 'lowest hem.'

The antithesis between Heidegger's interpretation of Kant and Herrigel's indeed provides us with what is of utmost importance for our issue: the acute either/or present in Kant between a metaphysics of finitude and a metaphysics of infinity. The problem

197. Herrigel, 83.
198. Herrigel, 19.
199. Herrigel, 25ff.
200. *'Konform'-sein.*—Trans.
201. Herrigel, 36.
202. Herrigel, 107f., 112f.

is refined to the point that it already signifies the pure objective line of inquiry[203]. Thus, it is already staring the answer in the face. Both [types of metaphysics] will be emphasized below.

*

We will (with Hugo Dingler) probably be able to say quite generally that metaphysics is concerned with the 'last or ultimate'[204]. The purely bibliographical term 'meta phusica'—i.e., the writings that come *after* the *Physics* in the catalog of Aristotle's writings—then inwardly turns into an objective one: what is 'last' in all questions that can be posed about reality. Objectively, this 'last' is for Aristotle at the same time the 'first'; indeed, it is 'first' before it is 'last.'[205] For Plato, subjectively and methodologically the 'first' is prior, while for Aristotle, subjectively and methodologically the 'last' is prior. Plato's metaphysics is an a priori metaphysics that immediately inquires into the 'first' and 'last' and only then examines 'the derived'[206] (the *metechonta*) in light of them. The metaphysics of Aristotle is an a posteriori metaphysics, which initially explores sensory reality (in the *phusica*) before then (*meta [ta] phusica*) posing the question about the 'first' and 'last' indirectly through this sensory reality.

In this sense, metaphysics can be defined in its broadest terms: it concerns the 'last.' Therefore, we will preserve the full incisiveness of our inquiry by framing all our previous findings under the concept of the 'last.'

For the *critical metaphysics of finitude*, 'the Nothing' is this 'last.' For finitude qua finitude is (in its specific contrast to 'Is')

203. *Sach-Fragestellung.*—Trans.

204. *das 'Letzte.'* There is a subtle, recurring wordplay in the German between different senses of *Letzte*, either as 'last' in a series or as 'most fundamental.' I have rendered it 'last' below in an attempt to retain Przywara's deliberate wordplay describing the object of metaphysics as 'the first and the last.' But the reader should keep in mind that by 'last' he also means something like 'most fundamental' or 'ultimate,' both senses of which are conveyed in the German word *'Letzte.'*—Trans.

205. See p. 87f. above.

206. *das 'Abgeleitete.'*—Trans.

the 'is not' of the perpetual flux of 'was' and 'will (be).' From this (immanent) ground, finitude expands to the 'infinite intensity' of its 'drive toward the infinite.' It is thus (within the framework of a closed finitude) a 'productive Nothing.' This means, logically, as Heidegger puts it: "Ex nihilo omne ens qua ens fit [From the nothing all beings as beings come to be]."[207]

The formal *act* of metaphysics then is: to stand in the formal ground of finitude as such and therefore 'to-hold-itself-into-the-Nothing.' In this formal act, the formal *object* of metaphysics is then grasped: the objective formal ground of finitude as such, i.e., the Nothing. But it is grasped insofar as it is the 'first' and 'last,' that is, as the *nihilum, ex quo omne ens qua ens fit,* i.e., as the Nothing of infinite intensity [that tends] toward 'is,' and [which is a] productive intensity. For 'from' it 'all being' 'comes to be.' Held out into the Nothing, the act of metaphysics subjectively encompasses all being because objectively, Dasein's "being held out into the nothing" "is its surpassing of beings as a whole. It is transcendence."[208]

With this, however, the 'last' of this metaphysics of finitude is the identity of its last act and object[209]: i.e., the Parmenidean last of *to auto* of *noein* (the act of metaphysics) and *einai* (the object of metaphysics). The "holding-itself-into-the-Nothing" (as an act of the metaphysics of finitude)—to the extent that it concerns an inner standing within the Nothing in order to "surpass being as a whole" from there—is to be one[210] with this Nothing. However, since the objective, radical Nothing precedes this subjective unity[211], the final conclusion follows from Heidegger's proposition that the understanding of being is self-understanding, i.e., being's self-disclosure. This conclusion applies Parmenidean

207. Heidegger, *Was ist Metaphysik?*, 26. [Heidegger, *What is Metaphysics?*, 108.]
208. Heidegger, 24. [Heidegger, *What is Metaphysics?*, 106.]
209. *Akt- und Gegenstand-Letzten.*—Trans.
210. *ein Eins-sein.*—Trans.
211. *Eins-sein.*—Trans.

identity to the metaphysics of finitude: in the act of metaphysics (of finitude), 'finitude as such' expresses itself as 'finite as such,' i.e., the objective Nothing (as the immanent formal ground of finitude) manifests itself as nothingness[212]. Not only (as Heidegger himself explains in *Was ist Metaphysik?*) does 'nihilation,' i.e., negation[213], point back to the 'Nothing.' Rather, logically the essence of the metaphysics of finitude lies in the self-disclosure of (objective) Nothing in the (subjective) nihilation, but a Nothing and negation from which everything positive emerges 'toward infinity,' i.e., the productive Nothing in the productive nihilation: the divinity of the self-identity of the productive Nothing.

The reverse is true for the *critical metaphysics of infinity*. Certainly, finitude is specifically an 'is not.' But inasmuch as everything finite in its 'was' and 'will (be)' still always 'is,' it is rather a received 'is' from an absolute 'Is.' Therefore, the first and last is this 'Is.' Finitude is an 'is' not in the sense of a 'toward infinity' from Nothing toward the (immanent) Is, but rather through the self-communication of a (transcendent) infinite Is toward Nothing. Heidegger's statement "Ex nihilo omne ens qua ens fit"[214] is opposed by another statement, "Ex Ipso Esse omne ens qua ens fit."[215]

Consequently, the formal *act* of metaphysics means: to stand in the effective ground[216] of finitude as a whole. This is the Platonic ἐπιστήμη, which, in contrast to the *doxa* of the empirical sciences, is binding for the act of metaphysics. In Kantian terms, it means to stand in the 'categorical truth' demanded for metaphysics, to stand in original 'truth as such,' as (in Herrigel's terms) the 'within us' of the original-creative 'pure knowledge.' But since

212. *nichtshaft.*—Trans.
213. *"Nichtung," d.h. die Verneinung.*—Trans.
214. Every being comes to be as such from the Nothing.—Trans.
215. Every being comes to be as such from Being Itself.—Trans.
216. *Wirk-Grund.*—Trans.

this "pure knowledge" is the "source of all being,"[217] it is further evident how in this 'to stand in . . .' as the object of metaphysics, this 'source of all being' manifests itself, insofar as it "creates worlds in original syntheses,"[218] i.e., the *infinitum actuale*, as it is 'toward' the *infinitum potentiale* within an infinity of possibilities (in an *infinitum relationale*).

With this, however, the most fundamental Parmenidean *identity* is finally expressed: the *to auto* between the absolute *noein* (in the 'unconditionally true' of the act of metaphysics) and the absolute *einai* (of the 'source of all being' in the object of metaphysics). If the act of metaphysics is fundamentally the 'within us' of pure original knowledge, which is the 'source of all being,' then this act is, in its ultimate sense, the self-revelation of the ontic Is in the noetic Is ('unconditional truth'). The 'last' of the metaphysics of infinity is therefore this identity: the objective Is in its noetically existing self-disclosure[219]. By being in its very essence the 'source of all being' and expressing itself in its self-disclosure within finite understanding, by being in its self-identity 'self-communicative' toward finitude, whence this finitude (qua finitude) is from this self-communication and exists by it, in it, and from it—insofar as [all this is the case,] the supreme antithesis to the divinity of the self-identity of the productive Nothing is achieved: the divinity of the self-identity of the self-communicating Is.

We have thus delineated the antithesis between Heidegger's Kant and Herrigel's Kant to the point that it has reached the objective level of the problem of metaphysics in general. It is thus automatically subject to consideration at this level. Which is to say, we have acquired the inherent right to examine the Kantian antithesis between the metaphysics of finitude and the metaphysics of infinity in the objective phenomenon[220] itself. It is the path

217. Herrigel, *Die metaphysische Form*, 185.
218. Herrigel, 37.
219. *das objective Ist in seiner noetisch ist-haften Selbst-Aussage.*—Trans.
220. *Sach-Phänomen.*—Trans.

on which the Kantian approach changes into the Thomistic one of a *metaphysics of the analogia entis*.

We begin with the problem of the *act* of metaphysics.

It is undoubtedly true—as asserted here by the metaphysics of infinity—that the act of metaphysics concerns 'unconditional truth.' For when it pertains, objectively, to the 'first' and 'last' (from which everything originates and toward which everything converges), it also relates, correlatively, to a fundamental certainty, the most unconditional 'thus and not otherwise.' Therefore, Plato demands *epistēmē* for the act of metaphysics; Aristotle, the precision of the syllogism; and Kant, pure apriority. Which is to say, the act of metaphysics requires a noetic Is: absolute truth.

On the other hand—and in this respect, the metaphysics of finitude also has its justification—this very act of metaphysics is the act of the created human being. If he relates to the first and the last in this act, he must evidently stand in that inner 'last' of his own being, in which the question of the first and last immediately arises. However, this innermost last is his peculiar 'is and yet is not,' in such a way that the 'is not' in this formula is the last of the last. For everything that 'is' only ever 'comes to' the human being. No 'is' in the course of his existence guarantees a further 'is.' Every 'is' in itself has 'come.' Thus, the distinctive quality of the human being (and of every creature) resides in the 'is' itself, in the 'not' which this 'is' has 'received,' and the coming 'receives,' 'if or when' it 'comes.' If we transfer this understanding from the ontic to the noetic level, this is to say: the created human being (qua created human being) relates internally to that 'unconditional truth'—with which the act of metaphysics is concerned—to the extent that he stands noetically in his 'receptive (noetic) not.'

Therefore, first and foremost, the objectively necessary proposition results: the human, created act of metaphysics stands in the 'unconditional truth' that is impersonally and objectively[221]

---

221. *sachlich objektiv.*—Trans.

fitting for this act (thus the noetic absolute of the metaphysics of infinity) to the extent that it personally and subjectively[222] stands in the 'receptive not' (thus the noetic Nothing of the metaphysics of finitude).

But—second—this proposition can be interpreted neither within the framework of a metaphysics of infinity nor within that of a metaphysics of finitude. Both sides remain integral to the objective phenomenon[223] of the act of metaphysics: unconditional truth and receptive (noetic) 'not.' In a closed metaphysics of infinity, however, an internal derivation of receptive (noetic) 'not' from unconditional truth occurs. The metaphysical act of the human being is here simply the immediate 'within us' of absolute truth itself: the theophany of *Deus-Veritas*. Conversely, in a closed metaphysics of finitude, there is an internal derivation of unconditional truth from receptive (noetic) 'not.' The noetic Nothing is productive here. Unconditional truth is the upper horizon of the infinite intensity of this productivity. Both metaphysics thus contradict the simple objective phenomenon. They each sacrifice one side for the other.

Therefore—third—the objective phenomenon itself, in its inherent irreducibility, presents the solution. Unconditional truth manifests itself within the receptive 'not.' It thus appears, on the one hand, truly. The 'not' 'has' unconditional truth's 'Is,' has 'truth' in this 'Is.' There is a supreme unity between the two: 'tanta similitudo.'[224] On the other hand, amidst this, the fact remains that the 'Is' of unconditional truth is never the 'not.' In its self-communication, unconditional truth casts it shadow upward as the positive inexhaustibility of the noetic *infinitum actuale*, while in reception, the receptive 'not' casts its shadow downward

222. *persönlich subjektiv.*—Trans.
223. *Sach-Phänomen.*—Trans.
224. 'Tanta similitudo' is a textual allusion to the Fourth Lateran Council's teaching on analogy. Przywara continues the allusion below with his reference to the 'maior dissimilitudo.'—Trans.

as the negative possibility[225] of the noetic *infinitum potentiale*. The difference between the two becomes truly apparent when both attain to the highest unity in the act of metaphysics: 'maior dissimilitudo.' But that is the essence of the *analogia entis*: within the 'tanta similitudo,' the 'maior dissimilitudo.' Therefore, the essence of the act of metaphysics, starting from the pure objective phenomenon, is called: *noetic analogia entis*.

Let's move on to the problem of the *object* of metaphysics.

It is certainly true—as the metaphysics of infinity consistently asserts here—that the object of metaphysics is the 'first' and 'last' as the 'source of all being.' It concerns comprehending the grounded (the becoming world) from its ground.[226] Thus, it is ultimately about comprehending the ground, which is an understanding of the 'whence' of the grounded—that is, ideally, an understanding of the grounded 'from its ground.' In this sense, Platonism speaks of the inherent conditioning[227] between *ontōs on* and *mē on* as the ultimate structure of being; likewise, Aristotelianism speaks of the interplay between form and matter, and more consistently (because we are concerned here with the positive primal ground, from which everything originates and toward which everything converges), Thomas speaks of *Ipsum Esse* as the first and last. Just as, in the act of metaphysics, it concerns the noetic Is (absolute truth), so here, correspondingly, it logically pertains to the ontic Is (as the primal ground of every received 'is' of the becoming world).

On the other hand—and in this respect, the metaphysics of finitude also has its justification—this ontic Is (as object) is observed in that objectivity, which represents the formal 'whence' and 'whither' of grounded being to the ground of its being. If the ontic Is is seen as the 'first' and 'last' of the becoming

---

225. *Möglichkeit.*—Trans.

226. *Es geht um das Begreifen des Begründeten (der werde-haften Welt) von ihrem Grund her.*—Trans.

227. *Bedingtheit.*—Trans.

world's being[228], it is thus formally seen in the 'being seen' of this 'becoming-ness'[229]—i.e., in the 'is [and] is not' that constitutes this becoming-ness, and therefore distinctively in its 'is not,' which as such is completely receptive (the particular 'is' from the Is). The ontic Is is therefore seen as the object of metaphysics to the extent that this ultimate receptive (ontic) 'not' of the world is seen—i.e., to the extent that the knowing human is so immersed 'in the world' that he stands in its ultimate, specific 'not,' which alone relates directly to the Is.

Thus, first (correlative to the problem of the act), the proposition emerges: the human, created act of metaphysics impersonally and objectively stands before its required object—the ontic Is as the 'source of all being' (thus, the ontic Absolute of the metaphysics of infinity)—to the extent that it personally and subjectively stands before the objective, receptive 'not' as the depth of the objective world (thus, before the ontic Nothing of the metaphysics of finitude).

But—second—this proposition (like the corresponding one in the problem of the act) cannot be interpreted either within the framework of a metaphysics of infinity or within that of a metaphysics of finitude. Both sides remain integral to the objective phenomenon of the object of metaphysics: ontic Is and receptive (ontic) 'not.' In a closed metaphysics of infinity, however, an internal derivation of receptive (ontic) 'not' from the ontic Is occurs. What is immediately personally and subjectively present to humans as an object—ultimate, receptive (ontic) 'not' in the essence of the world—is here simply the immediate 'here and now' of the ontic Is in the 'appearance' of the communicated 'is': the theophany of *Deus-Esse*. Conversely, in a closed metaphysics of finitude, there is an internal derivation of the ontic Is from receptive (ontic) 'not.' The ontic Nothing is 'productive,' and the

228. *werde-haften Welt-Seins.*—Trans.
229. *Werde-haftigkeit.*—Trans.

ontic Is is the upper horizon of its creative being[230]. 'Ens qua ens' emanates from it. Therefore, in its infinite intensity, it is the 'ontic Is *in fieri*.' Both metaphysics thus contradict the simple, objective phenomenon. They each sacrifice one side for the other.

Therefore—third—here too (as in the problem of the act), the objective phenomenon itself, in its inherent irreducibility, is the solution. The ontic Is (as the 'source of all being') is truly and effectively in receptive (ontic) 'not.' As the world continually 'is,' in this 'is' it is truly the self-manifestation of the Is, from which, in which, and toward which the 'is' is. In the 'is,' 'not' 'has' the Is. Thus, there is the highest unity between them: (ontic) 'tanta similitudo.' On the other hand, amidst this, the fact remains that this Is is never the 'not.' In its self-communication, the ontic Is casts its shadow upward as the positive inexhaustibility of the ontic *infinitum actuale*, while in reception, receptive (ontic) 'not' casts its shadow downward as the negative possibility of ontic *infinitum potentiale*. The difference between the two becomes truly apparent when both attain to the highest unity in the object of metaphysics (the 'is' of 'not' from the Is): (ontic) 'maior dissimilitudo.' But that is the essence of the *analogia entis*: within the 'tanta similitudo,' the 'maior dissimilitudo.' Therefore, the essence of the object of metaphysics, starting from the pure objective phenomenon, is called: *ontic analogia entis*.

Now only the implications for the *problem of identity* remain, as they finally emerged within the metaphysics of infinity and finitude respectively as the ultimate 'last.'

We must, according to the double *analogia entis*, first say: Identity in the earlier sense has ceased to exist. It exists only for the relationship between the noetic and ontic Is. The Is qua Is is the *tauto* [identity] of *noein* (*veritas absoluta*) and *einai* (*esse absolutum*). To express it more fully, in the sense of ancient transcendentalism, which encompasses truth, goodness, and beauty

---

230. *Sein-Schaffen.*—Trans.

within *noien*: the Is as Is is the essential identity of absolute truth, goodness, and beauty with absolute being.

Second, it is also not possible to establish an identity in a derived sense—namely, between the noetic and ontic 'not.' For the relationship of the *analogia entis*, in which both stand in relation to the noetic and ontic Is, does not allow for a separation. It is part of the concept of noetic and ontic Is that noetic and ontic 'not' is possible only as originating from it, although as distinct from it: as a peculiarity of the 'communicated' within the communicated 'is.' 'No' ultimately arises from 'yes,' although in no way as an 'appearing' 'yes.' In this sense, Thomas Aquinas put the matter quite profoundly when he said that 'matter in general' (the *negative infinitum potentiale* of the 'is not') is 'co-created' by God since something 'other than God' is differentiated from God by its inner 'not,' and so can only be created by God 'thus.'

Third, it is also not possible to establish an identity between the noetic *analogia entis* (in the act of metaphysics) and the ontic *analogia entis* (as the object of metaphysics). For: if we take the *analogia entis* in its objective sense, both noetically and ontically, its tendency proceeds 'from top to bottom,' since it fundamentally concerns the mystery of the self-communication of the noetic and ontic Is. A *tauto* between *noein* and *einai* would therefore be the expanded *tauto* between the noetic and ontic Is: God's self-identity, even in his self-communication. However, if we consider the *analogia entis*, as it subjectively and methodologically presents itself in the approach of metaphysics, it is inherently 'unclosable' in its tendency 'from below to above.' Both the noetic and the ontic *analogia entis*, by virtue of the 'maior dissimilitudo,' culminate in the transcendent incomprehensibility of the Is. An 'identity' here would presuppose that from the creature's perspective, the (noetic as well as ontic) God-creature correlation would be 'comprehensible.' However, then God would be contained in the formula of this correlation, would be encompassed, and thus would not be God. The Is would be mastered by the 'not' and so would not be the Is.

Fourth, 'analogy' considered as the 'last' remains negative initially, inasmuch as in its logical consistency (as we just saw), any Parmenidean identity is excluded from metaphysics at the outset. However, it also manifests itself positively in a certain ultimate sense in the relationship between the act of metaphysics (noetic *analogia entis*) and the object of metaphysics (ontic *analogia entis*). For it is not the case (which would establish an identity once more) that the object of metaphysics would present itself in a pure self-reflection of the act of metaphysics: being [revealed] within the truth, the ontic *analogia entis* within the noetic. Rather, the created act is essentially directed away from itself toward something, and only then [in a second moment] does it turn back to itself from this something. The created act is primarily 'intentional' and only secondarily 'reflexive.' Thus, the view of truth arises in and from the view of being, and, consequently, the view of the noetic *analogia entis* arises in and from that of the ontic *analogia entis*. So, in the relationship between the act and the object of metaphysics itself, the 'movement away from itself, beyond itself' characteristic of the *analogia entis* becomes evident. It is a possession of 'being' (the ontic *analogia entis*) in 'truth' (the noetic *analogia entis*), in that the act of truth reaches beyond itself toward being—i.e., in that it is conscious of the transcendence of being. But if transcendence implies a 'being-beyond,' we then have the formula: 'being' is 'in' 'truth,' in that it is 'beyond' it. But that is the form of the 'maior dissimilitudo' within the 'tanta similitudo.' That is, the metaphysics of the *analogia entis* is so thoroughly shaped by the form of analogy that even its internal relationship between act and object bears this form.

A Prospect
John Henry Newman

It should be clear by now how the two major tendencies discussed at the beginning of our study have worked their way through all the problems we have surveyed. However, this leads to a final question that, much like the initial theme, can only be presented in broad outlines: If Thomas's solution emerges from all of Kant's problems, in what sense, then, can there be a resurrection of Thomas?

Is the only possible characterization of Aquinas one where his philosophy and theology resemble to no small degree the artistic world of his fellow Dominican Fiesole,[1] both of whose clearly drawn lines are transfigured, elevated out of the chaos of concrete life? To ask the question is already to provide the answer. For the Church herself places the great 'doctor communis,' as the formulary for his feast day says, 'in medio ecclesiae'—i.e., amidst the starkly, individually differentiated variety of her other great teachers, such as the volcanic Jerome or the noble Anselm of Canterbury. And she places him, in a very special sense, alongside the saint she almost celebrates as the incomparably greater. That is, she places the Dominican friar—who was removed from all the pressures of worldly life from the outset—alongside Augustine, the ardent seeker of God who rose only with anguish from the confusion of the world.

So, the Church herself does not forbid us should we prefer to listen to a 'voice of wisdom' amidst the fractured riddles of modernity—riddles that only find their unsettling expression, if not their resolution, in Kant's tragic solution. Again, the Church does not forbid us should we prefer to listen to someone who, in all honesty, sees himself only as a faithful disciple of Aquinas, yet

1. I.e., Fra Angelico.—Trans.

is an heir to his wisdom through a life of restless seeking and who therefore imparts Thomas's wisdom to us in the language of Augustine. Of course, I am speaking of the Augustine of our modern times, *John Henry Cardinal Newman.*

First, Newman's entire line of inquiry arose from the problem for which Kant had no solution but tragic unity. His youth itself was permeated by the irreconcilable antitheses that, only in a more continental form, presented themselves to the philosopher from Königsberg. On the one side lay the rationalism of the logicians as encountered by the young student at Oxford. [Richard] Whately is an example of this. On the other side lay Hume's empiricist skepticism, something Newman genuinely wrestled with. Again, on one side lay the rationalist theology of reason, present in Anglican theology itself, against which the leader of the Tractarians wrote in his Catholic letters in the *Tracts for the Times.* On the other side lay the religious irrationalism of the 'religion of feeling' kindled by Coleridge and the revivalist sects, against which the preacher of St. Mary's did not tire of fighting and in response to which his own path of development within Anglicanism increasingly led to the strictest dogmatic religion.

Thus, on the one hand (in response to philosophical antitheses), his inquiry arises concerning the relationship between conceptual thought and its form of certainty (notional thought) and experiential thought and its form of certainty (real thought). But similarly (in response to theological antitheses), his inquiry arises between a more insightful faith of ideal dogmatic connections and a more vital faith of blind surrender to the God of incomprehensibility who alone 'sees.' And just as the works conducted by the Anglican (the *Oxford University Sermons*) or by the Catholic (the *Discourses to Mixed Congregations, Idea of a University,* and *Grammar of Assent*) not only complement each other in their particular lines of inquiry and in the tendency of their responses but also demonstrate the vitality of his ceaseless questioning even into old age, so too do the diaries of the Anglican from his Oxford days and the final philosophical-theological sketches of the aged Oratorian of Birmingham converge on the same point: the relentless quest toward unfathomable mysteries. He is the Augustinian seeker of truth in modern times.

Newman is also, second, the Augustinian seeker of truth in modern times who trod the essential paths of Aquinas.

His response to the philosophical question concerning the problem of knowledge is twofold: [1] the theory of the ordered relationship between the pure thought of immediate experience, which indeed has the advantage of proximity to things, but the disadvantage of only providing a partial account for the connections between things, and [2] the pure thought of concepts. While the latter mode of thinking avoids the shortcomings of the former by offering an explicit account of itself, it trades away the advantage of proximity to things for the disadvantage of lesser proximity to them. Since conceptual (*notionale*) thinking is presented as an explication (explicit reason) of experiential (real) thinking (implicit reason), they are one in the living unity of the thinking personality, as well as in the enduring nature of the truth conceived. But what is this if not the revival of the fundamental idea of Thomas Aquinas's epistemology in a modern context? For Thomas, is not thinking first of all internally bound to the proximity of the fully concrete world of experience, to the extent that his axiom declares "nihil in intellectu quod non fuerit in sensu"[2]? Yet, at the same time, does not thinking as an analytic-synthetic process imply an abstraction of the internal connections that are only implicitly contained in the unity of simple, lived experience? And is not his other axiom, "agere sequitur esse"[3], that such unity of experience and pure thought ultimately reveals itself as an expression of the essence of the living human being?[4] And doesn't

2. nothing is in the intellect that was not [first] in the senses.—Trans.
3. action follows being.—Trans.
4. Thomas Aquinas, *De Veritate* 2.6 ad 3.

this unity of experience and thought also express the "unum esse" of the formal unity of spirit-soul and body? And yet again, through this unity of person, doesn't the unity of experience and thought also express the essence of truth, which appears twofold within the creature, on the side of receiving from things and on the side of the creativity of thought?[5]

We will probably have to say the same when we examine Newman's answer to the question of the nature of man and the world. It is characterized by a duality. The first is the motif of 'change,' which is expressed most forcefully in his two statements "My unchangeableness here below is perseverance in changing" and "To be perfect is to have changed often."[6] While the first statement comes toward the end of his life, the second is found in the work that marks the pivotal midpoint of his life—*The Development of Christian Doctrine*. This motif is the confession of the fundamental state of becoming and therefore changeability of the creature, which ultimately has in it a relative unchangeability, in that it (in the knowledge and living acceptance of the depth of this changeability) becomes the pliant and malleable tool in the hand of the Unchangeable One: "Oh, support me, as I proceed in this great, awful, happy change, with the grace of Thy unchangeableness!" as Newman rightly prays.[7] The world and changeable humanity in the unchangeable God—this is the primary feature of Newman's worldview.

The second feature represents something like a darker shading of the first. In it, 'change' as a phenomenon of the fading transience of the sub-spiritual world is differentiated from 'change' as

---

5. Thomas Aquinas, *De Veritate* 1.9.

6. The first citation is from Newman, *Meditations and Devotions of the Late Cardinal Newman* (London: Longmans, Green, 1911), 370. The second is from *The Development of Christian Doctrine*, 6th ed. (Notre Dame, IN: University of Notre Dame Press, 1989), 40. I have supplied the original quotations by Newman rather than re-translating them out of Przywara's German back into English. Przywara has rendered them thus: "Meine Unwandelbarkeit hier auf Erden ist ständige Wandlung" and "Vollkommen sein heißt sich häufig gewandelt haben."—Trans.

7. Newman, *Meditations and Devotions*, 370. "Erhalte mich in dieser geheimnisvollen Wandlung durch die Gnade Deiner Unwandelbarkeit."—Trans.

a phenomenon of positive, dynamic life in the immortal spiritual world. For Newman, the world of spiritual life is the 'true' world, so that for the dreaming gaze of the young person, as well as, to some extent, for the seclusion of the old man, the sub-spiritual world fades away like an insubstantial, fluttering veil to the world of spirit. He is the thinker of a constant yearning for a pure life of the spirit, although (or, indeed, perhaps because) his senses possessed a heightened sensitivity to the colorful abundance of the visible world in all its extent. But we ask again: Is Newman's 'change' not a true revival of the 'actus in potentia,' the dynamic nature of becoming ('être dynamogénique' [dynamogenic being] or 'devenir' [becoming], as recent Thomists say), of Aquinas's metaphysics? And doesn't Newman's emphasis on the spirit also have a true precedent in that aspect of the saint's metaphysics where the world appears as a downward 'materialization' of the spiritual, from the pure 'actus immaterialis' of angelic spirits to the 'formae materiales' of natural bodies? And doesn't this happen such that the realm of 'materia' (in its primal essence as 'materia prima') appears as 'pura potentialitas' in contrast to the 'actualitas' of the realm of spirits, as a being-less 'pure potentiality' contrasted with ontologically rich[8] 'pure actuality'? Considered thus, mustn't the world of matter then be regarded as 'unreal' in comparison to the world of forms and spirits as what is 'real'?

So, we come to the final point of agreement: in their image of God. Both Thomas and Newman emphasize God as the Incomprehensible through an increasing transcendence of the senses. For both, there is accentuation on the human aspect of our thinking—i.e., its connection to the senses. But for both, there is also the surging inclination toward the purely spiritual. In Thomas, this inclination is realized in the serene flight of contemplation; in Newman, in the painful melancholy of self-detachment. Thus, they both ultimately rest in the Spirit-God beyond all

8. *seinshaften.*—Trans.

comparisons: 'Deus tamquam ignotus' (Thomas), 'Incomprehensibleness' (Newman). Both the opposing tendencies from which our study proceeded are harmonized in a tranquil yet lively unity: the joyful contemplation of the eternal symbols[9] suspended in the awe of distance, but also the restless movement of creative life transformed into the serenity of worship before the One who alone is perfect—beyond reach, unattainable—for all eternity, surpassing all contentious striving for perfection. The 'incomprehensible God' frees the arms that cling tightly to Him in self-surrendering contemplation so that the creature may praise and glorify Him in liberated vitality. Yet He also lowers the lofty image of His primal perfection, which demands worship, into the soul wearied by life's struggle so that the humility of worship may be the 'inner freedom' of this life's vitality, its ability to find 'rest' in 'action.'

So, if we now survey our problem from Newman through Kant and Thomas back to Augustine, we find that the solution to the antithesis of the two tendencies that shape philosophy and theology lies in the One. It lies in the One, as Augustine expressed it in the words: "Quaeritur inveniendus, quia occultus est, et invenitur quaerendus, quia immensus est," "He is sought in order to be found, because he is hidden, and is found in order to be sought, because he is immense."[10] The contemplation that immerses itself in God and in God's world is, indeed, worship of God's greatness. But when it relinquishes the dynamic rhythm of 'seeking to find, and finding to seek' for a malignant grasping[11] (the 'anapausis' against which Augustine fought), it offers such scant worship to the 'ever greater God' that, instead, in this desire to merge into the original sin of "you will be like God,"[12] it plunges, having forsaken the reverence of 'standing at a distance' (see Exod. 3:5).

9. *Sinbilder* [sic]; read as *Sinnbilder*.—Trans.
10. See Augustine, *In Io. Tract.* 63.1.
11. *entlebendigtes Aufgehen.*—Trans.
12. See Gen. 3:5.—Trans.

True contemplation can only occur in the unclouded vitality of creaturely life. In this respect, the striving, dynamic life, directed toward God and within His world—the antithesis to the former tendency—is truly sustained by reverence before the towering immensity of God, whose inexhaustible depths precisely demand a constant 'seeking to find, and finding to seek' as an attitude of worship and love on the part of the creature. But when it adopts such a 'seeking to find, and finding to seek' mentality because it believes, in the inner universality of this disposition, that it can somehow exhaust the transcendent universality of God or even contain it within itself, it degenerates into a form of self-idolatry that is as bad as, or perhaps even worse than, the first tendency. The 'seeking to find, and finding to seek' of the movement of life is only genuine by virtue of the unchanging, unmoving act of humble submission before the truly transcendent God, who is "exalted above all things that exist or can be conceived beside him," as the Vatican Council says.[13] It is genuine through the intact 'quia' [because] of the explanatory clauses: "Because he (God) is hidden . . . , because he is immense."

That is the mysterious foundation for both the harmonious resolution of our question in Thomas and the tragic one in Kant, as well as the revitalization in Newman of Augustine's quest for God. It is faith in a God who is truly 'mystery' and 'immensity,' the faith of surrender and devotion to a God "ineffably exalted above all things that exist or can be conceived beside him." It is faith in the God of 'infinite perfection,' faith thus as unchanging unity with the Unchangeable. This faith, which seems to extinguish all movement of life, is precisely the innermost condition of universal movement, the movement of eternal life through the heights and depths of God's mysteries, fundamentally the movement of not-resting in full possession, the movement of 'seeking to find, and finding to seek.' For to find God is to find the ever-newly-discoverable, to grasp Him is to grasp the ungraspable,

13. Vatican I, *Dei Filius*, ch. 1, cited in Denzinger, 43rd ed., § 3001.—Trans.

to understand Him is to understand the incomprehensible—God who is 'ever greater' for eternity.

Bibliography

Diès, Auguste. *Autour de Platon: Essais de critique et d'histoire.* Vol. 2, *Les Dialogues–Esquisses doctrinales.* Paris: Beauchesne, 1927.

Eschweiler, Karl. *Die zwei Wege der neueren Theologie: Georg Hermes–Matth. Jos. Scheeben: Eine kritische Untersuchung des Problems der theologischen Erkenntnis.* Augsburg, DE: Benno Filser, 1926.

Heidegger, Martin. *Kant und das Problem der Metaphysik.* Bonn, DE: Friedrich Cohen, 1929. ET: *Kant and the Problem of Metaphysics,* Translated by Richard Taft. 5th ed. Bloomington, IN: Indiana University Press, 1997.

———. *Was ist Metaphysik?* Bonn, DE: Friedrich Cohen, 1929. ET: "What is Metaphysics?" In *Basic Writings,* edited by David Farrell Krell, 89–110. London: Harper, 2008.

Herrigel, Eugen. *Die metaphysische Form: eine Auseinandersetzung mit Kant.* Vol. 1, *Der mundus sensibilis.* Tübingen, DE: Mohr, 1929.

Kroner, Richard. *Von Kant bis Hegel.* 2 vols. Tübingen, DE: Mohr Siebeck, 1921–24.

Maréchal, Joseph. *De l'antiquité à la fin du moyen âge: La critique ancienne de la connaissance.* Vol. 1 of *Le point de départ de la Métaphysique: Leçons sur le développement historique et théorique du problème de la connaissance.* Bruges, BE: Beyaert, 1922.

———. *Le conflit du Rationalisme et de l'Empirisme dans la philosophie moderne, avant Kant.* Vol. 2 of *Le point de départ de la Métaphysique: Leçons sur le développement historique et théorique du problème de la connaissance.* Bruges, BE: Beyaert, 1923.

Maréchal, Joseph. *La Critique de Kant.* Vol. 3 of *Le point de départ de la Métaphysique: Leçons sur le développement historique et théorique du problème de la connaissance.* Bruges, BE: Beyaert, 1923.

———. *Le système idéaliste chez Kant et les postkantiens.* Vol. 4 of *Le point de départ de la Métaphysique: Leçons sur le développement historique et théorique du problème de la connaissance.* Brussels, BE: Universelle; Paris: Desclée du Brouwer, 1947.

———. *Le Thomisme devant la Philosophie critique.* Vol. 5 of *Le point de départ de la Métaphysique: Leçons sur le développement historique et théorique du problème de la connaissance.* Bruges, BE: Beyaert, 1926.

Newman, John Henry. *An Essay on the Development of Christian Doctrine.* 6th ed. Notre Dame, IN: University of Notre Dame Press, 1989.

———. *Meditations and Devotions of the Late Cardinal Newman.* London: Longmans, Green, 1911.

Przywara, Erich. *Ringen der Gegenwart: Gesammelte Aufsätze, 1922–1927.* Augsburg, DE: Benno Filser, 1929.

Sladeczek, F.M. "Das Widerspruchsprinzip und der Satz von hinreichenden Grunde." *Scholastik* 2 (1927): 1–37.

Thomas Aquinas. *Summa theologiae.* 8 vols. Translated by Laurence Shapcote. Edited by John Mortensen and Enrique Alarcón. Latin/English Edition of the Works of St. Thomas Aquinas 13–20. Lander, WY: Aquinas Institute, 2012.

———. *De Veritate.* ET: *Truth.* Vol. 1, *Questions I–IX.* Translated by Robert W. Mulligan. Chicago: Henry Regnery, 1952.

Index